Catherine Cookson was bor[...]
daughter of a poverty-stric[...]
believed to be her older siste[...]
eventually moved south to ~~Hastings where~~ she met and
married a local grammar-school master. At the age of forty
she began writing about the lives of the working-class people
with whom she had grown up, using the place of her birth as
the background to many of her novels.

Although originally acclaimed as a regional writer – her novel
The Round Tower won the Winifred Holtby award for the best
regional novel of 1968 – her readership soon began to spread
throughout the world. Her novels have been translated
into more than a dozen languages and more than
50,000,000 copies of her books have been sold in Corgi alone.
Ten of her novels have been made into successful television
dramas, and more are planned.

Catherine Cookson's many bestselling novels have established
her as one of the most popular of contemporary women
novelists. After receiving an OBE in 1985, Catherine
Cookson was created a Dame of the British Empire in 1993.
She and her husband Tom now live near Newcastle-upon-
Tyne.

As I look back on my life over the years, I seem always to
have been fighting to survive, and I wonder from where came
the strength that has enabled me still to be here. It certainly
isn't a physical power, nor does it come from the mind; so it
must come from the spirit, an intangible, elusive quality that
can only be described as a gift – but a gift that needs to be
used'
Catherine Cookson

BOOKS BY CATHERINE COOKSON

NOVELS

Kate Hannigan
The Fifteen Streets
Colour Blind
Maggie Rowan
Rooney
The Menagerie
Slinky Jane
Fanny McBride
Fenwick Houses
Heritage of Folly
The Garment
The Fen Tiger
The Blind Miller
House of Men
Hannah Massey
The Long Corridor
The Unbaited Trap
Katie Mulholland
The Round Tower
The Nice Bloke
The Glass Virgin
The Invitation
The Dwelling Place
Feathers in the Fire
Pure as the Lily
The Mallen Streak
The Mallen Girl
The Mallen Litter
The Invisible Cord
The Gambling Man
The Tide of Life
The Slow Awakening
The Iron Façade
The Girl

The Cinder Path
Miss Martha Mary Crawford
The Man Who Cried
Tilly Trotter
Tilly Trotter Wed
Tilly Trotter Widowed
The Whip
Hamilton
The Black Velvet Gown
Goodbye Hamilton
A Dinner of Herbs
Harold
The Moth
Bill Bailey
The Parson's Daughter
Bill Bailey's Lot
The Cultured Handmaiden
Bill Bailey's Daughter
The Harrogate Secret
The Black Candle
The Wingless Bird
The Gillyvors
My Beloved Son
The Rag Nymph
The House of Women
The Maltese Angel
The Year of the Virgins
The Golden Straw
Justice is a Woman
The Tinker's Girl
A Ruthless Need
The Obsession
The Upstart
The Branded Man

THE MARY ANN STORIES

A Grand Man
The Lord and Mary Ann
The Devil and Mary Ann
Love and Mary Ann

Life and Mary Ann
Marriage and Mary Ann
Mary Ann's Angels
Mary Ann and Bill

FOR CHILDREN

Matty Doolin
Joe and the Gladiator
The Nipper
Rory's Fortune
Our John Willie

Mrs Flannagan's Trumpet
Go Tell It To Mrs Golightly
Lanky Jones
Nancy Nutall and the Mongrel
Bill and the Mary Ann Shaughnessy

AUTOBIOGRAPHY

Our Kate
Catherine Cookson Country

Let Me Make Myself Plain
Plainer Still

PLAINER STILL

Catherine Cookson

CORGI BOOKS

PLAINER STILL
A CORGI BOOK : 0 552 14384 7

Originally published in Great Britain by Bantam Press,
a division of Transworld Publishers Ltd

PRINTING HISTORY
Bantam Press edition published 1995
Corgi edition published 1996

PHOTOGRAPHIC ACKNOWLEDGEMENTS
Page 6 top and bottom *Daily Express*/Brian Duff; pp. 7 and 8 *Newcastle
Chronicle and Journal*; p.9 top Allan Glenwright; p.9 bottom University of
Newcastle upon Tyne; p.10 top Camera Press/Allan Glenbrook; p.10 bottom
and p.11 Tyne and Wear Museums; p.12 top and bottom Photo-Mayo; p.14
top *Shields Gazette*/Jim Appleby; p.14 bottom *Shields Gazette*; p.15 top North
News and Pictures; p.15 bottom Jim Appleby; p.16 Mark Gerson.

All other photographs were provided by the author.

Set in 10½/12½ Linotype Sabon by
Phoenix Typesetting, Ilkley, West Yorkshire

Corgi Books are published by Transworld Publishers Ltd,
61–63 Uxbridge Road, London W5 5SA,
in Australia by Transworld Publishers (Australia) Pty Ltd,
15–25 Helles Avenue, Moorebank, NSW 2170,
and in New Zealand by Transworld Publishers (NZ) Ltd,
3 William Pickering Drive, Albany, Auckland.

Reproduced, printed and bound in Great Britain by
Cox & Wyman Ltd, Reading, Berks.

This is more than an anthology in that it exposes a personality to the core

PLAINER STILL

Contents

PART TWO – THE IN-BETWEEN

PART THREE – MY PRIVATE WAR

And Plainer Still

As I have said before, it took me twelve years to complete my autobiography, for I rewrote it eight times.

How long did it take me to write *Let Me Make Myself Plain*? Well, I spent six months just sorting out all the odd pieces of writing I had done during previous years right back to 1945, the year in which I had my breakdown. That, of course, wasn't taking into account the rewriting and editing.

In 1937, having given an acquaintance a piece of my work to read and been given his opinion not in words but in utter silence, I burnt all the scribblings I had carried around with me for years. Later, I realised how stupid I had been, because in destroying those first efforts I had lost some good material; henceforth I hung on to my bits and pieces of prose and what came under the mis-heading of poetry, which I later called 'Prose On Short Lines'.

I have explained in the foreword to *Let Me Make Myself Plain* how I came to write a series of epilogues for television, and then, through pressure from my secretary, my husband and my publisher, to spend another six months in sorting out the mass of material to compile the book.

Now, I like writing novels. I enjoy thinking up the story, talking it down onto tape, then meticulously going over and over the rough-typed script. I get tired, but it is a pleasurable tiredness. Not so with the sorting out of these bits and pieces, for this I found irritating in the extreme and nerve-racking: Was that worth putting in? Would this poem go with that piece of prose? No; it would have to be moved to so and so.

After weeks of work I had all the pieces numbered, but if I reshuffled those numbers once, I must have done so fifty times in the course of those six months. I became absolutely sick and tired of the whole business; and what certainly did not help was my husband's almost daily suggestions:

'Look,' he would say, sorting through another pile of oddments; 'this is a much better piece than the one you have put in as number fifteen.'

Or, 'Look; I would move that poem to fit number seven and move them both back towards the end of the book,' followed by many pages being flicked over, and then, 'Why not put them in here, next to your seascape painting?' . . .

The climax came the afternoon when, after weeks and weeks of sorting and re-sorting and rewriting and on the point of exhaustion, I said, 'That's that! Thank God.' It was when the schoolmaster husband who had been reading through them once again said, 'I really do think that you should alter that line in such and such a poem, it just doesn't scan,' that the bubble burst.

It was in the summer, so there was no fire in the grate. I can assure you, if there had been, that completed script would have gone into it, even though, being of a logical mind, I would know that

that act of defiance could be rectified by again going through the various copies upstairs in the office; and I also knew that had the flames been beckoning I would have flown up there, grabbed the lot and consigned them to the ultimate end. Being unable to do this, the tearing up of the main script would have achieved nothing, and so, tossing the papers right and left, I bellowed, 'It's not going! It isn't worth printing. I'm sick and tired of the sight of it. Damn it! . . . and you.'

The fact that I'd already written eighty books and never lost my temper over a completed script, nor wanted it consigned to hell's flames, must say something about the effect the compilation of that book had on me.

A fortnight later, after another reshuffle, Paul Scherer, Alan Earney and Mark Barty-King came up from Bantam. They had heard of my recent reactions. They stood around the dining table and viewed the layout of the book, and they couldn't have been more enthusiastic.

But when I said to them, 'It's something entirely different, is it really *worth publishing*?' Alan has told me since, from the look on my face, they decided that the wisest thing was to get it out of my sight as quickly as possible. And this they did.

By this time, my attitude was: Let them get on with it. I couldn't care less. It won't go.

It is odd to me now, but I couldn't see any merit in it, and this feeling worried me, for there I was on the phone again saying to Alan, 'Look, do you think it will work? People want stories, something they can get their teeth into; that's all bits and pieces; and anyway, who wants to know about my war with God? And the whole, I feel, is trite in parts. I'm not happy about it.'

Tom knew how I felt and was forever reassuring me. But I wasn't to be placated.

Then came the day when I received the first book off the press, and there I was on the cover standing straight with the most sanctimonious look on my face. Oh, that nearly finished me. That wasn't me. Had I ever looked like that? Had I ever posed for that photo? Lord! that just finished it off.

I flicked through the pages and saw that Bantam had done a splendid job in their presentation. My paintings had come up well; the whole layout of the book was good; but what about the material? I couldn't bear to read one line.

Within a few weeks after publication I think Tom must have read that book twenty times, that is without exaggeration. He even sat up half of one night perusing it. Time and again he would exclaim on some new merit in it.

It is my habit when I have a new book out to give a copy to several of my friends. Yet, over the years I cannot recall one of them ever getting on the phone straightaway and saying, 'Oh, I've read it and enjoyed it, Catherine, and I think it's splendid.' That is, with the exception of David Harle, my then doctor, who not only tells me when he likes my work, but certainly when he doesn't like it. No; my friends had remained mute. So, what did I expect when handing out *Let Me Make Myself Plain*? Certainly not the reaction I received. If any, I had expected it to be, 'Yes; it's a nice little book.

Different from your usual stuff.'

How I detest that word 'nice'. You can get rigged out in your very best and you know that your best spells taste and some kind friend will say, 'Yes; you look very nice.' Or they will look at a painting that you've done and if the reaction is other than silence, it could be and has been, 'Yes; it'll be nice when it's framed.'

But what was their reaction to *Let Me Make Myself Plain*? Well, to me it was amazing. I can say three-quarters of them phoned up within two days with such remarks as, 'This is the best thing, I think, you've ever done.' Others, 'You do get to the bottom of things, don't you? It's most enlightening.' And others still, 'Oh, I've enjoyed the poems. Really, I never knew you wrote poetry.'

At this stage I recalled some years ago getting a phone call from a lady who said, 'I know you write your books but would you mind telling me, please, who writes your poems for you?'

I fully understand the feeling of the bull when he sees the red rag.

Anyway, this was only the beginning. The letters began coming in now and I had to ask myself yet again, Had I ever set out with the intention that my writings should carry a message? No; nor did I ever think that what I wrote could affect another person's life. Oh, no; never that. Or help someone's relative to die peacefully. The letters I received were simply beautiful and so touching that they brought tears to my eyes, and to Tom's, as on one morning when he was reading my mail to me – he does this because my eyesight is going – and he was halfway through this

19

particular letter when his voice broke and he said, 'I can't go on;' and he got up and walked away.

People are wonderfully kind, wonderfully appreciative. Knowing now how this book had been received, why was I so worried about it? Why did I not think it worthy of publication? I imagine it must have been because I was once again baring my soul, leaving myself naked to the world, and asking myself, Was that a good thing or a bad thing? Was I just using my pen to ease my mind, to get rid of my torturous thinking? Yes, perhaps it was this; but definitely it was not with the intention of putting over a message.

This being the case, why am I still at it? Why am I once more stripping my mind? Well, perhaps this time I'm not so much stripping my mind as opening doors in others, and in doing so letting them know they are not alone in their fears, and quirks, or in their searching. As I see it, we are all in the station waiting for the same train, and it will take on all colours and creeds, and there's only one passenger class, and the conductor is no collector of status tickets.

PART ONE

Thee and Me

Thee And Me

There's only thee and me,
That's all.
Yes, there are a few friends,
And acquaintances by the score;
There are publishers and agents,
And, what is more,
There are doctors galore;
But when all's said and done,
There's only thee and me.

Fifty-eight years ago
When I first saw you
I knew
There was only thee and me;
And you felt the same.
How do you think it came about?
Was it planned
That in all the land
Two odd bods like us should meet,
Marry, and stand the traumatic racket of years,
Never straining to be free?
Somebody, somewhere,
Must have willed there was only
Me for thee,
And thee for me.

Subconsciousness

I was very ill when I muttered the following into the tape and it took much longer than it had taken to read, and Tom says there was much more at the beginning that couldn't be made out – the whole was just murmured as if through delirium.

It is very strange but it is always when I'm in a low state that I write in this way.

The light filters through the trees from the far hill. I lie watching it, my body inert, still. Once it would have given me the urge to do my short lines, but now my mind, too, like my limbs, is still.

How long have I lain here in this state that is like the awaiting of death? Going down: all emotions gone: no looking back in bitterness: no hate, not even love in this deflative state.

The light still flickers through the trees although through sleet and rain now. The scene has changed but I remain the same, listless, without constructive thought. Always in the past, when ill, my mind has accelerated like a mill wheel, the waters running fast; but now all thoughts limp from my brain with time between them: no reasoning magic cries out for paper and pen. My mind like my body is almost at a standstill.

Sue lies beside me; she, too, is ill. We suffer from

the same complaint in which the past is a mountain weighing us down. Does she remember being thrown down the sewer, clinging for dear life to the last rung? Very likely, for she clings to her new security. I am now her last rung, as Tom is mine.

The light through the trees has changed yet again; the far hill is laced in white, there will be thick snow tonight and a white world tomorrow.

The scene is suddenly wild, the snow, wind-driven, has covered the pane. No longer does the light come through the trees, the hill is gone, the room is encased as if in a feathered tick in which I lie, still inert. Would that storm would rage within my mind and blow away this overpowering lassitude that lies upon me like a sheath, mistakenly bought before my time. Yet, what is my time? Is it now? I don't know. I can only wait until tomorrow, and if I wake to a white world then I shall know that yesterday was not the time to go.

A lot of birds will die tonight.
Where will they go?
Perhaps to join Simon, Sandy and Sue.

The Difficult Word

I'm sorry;
How difficult it is to say.
I find it so,
I always have:
Why should I say I'm sorry
When I'm right?
And how can I say such words
When I'm hot inside with rage
And indignation
Because I'm RIGHT?

And how can HE say
He's SORRY straightaway?
I'm incensed still more;
His humility makes me sore
And a lesser being
Because by this he seems to score.

When the fire slowly dies down
And there are no more
Recriminations to burn
I'm brought low further still
By realising
I've yet a lot to learn how, on my part,
To say I'm sorry with a contrite heart.

The Cinder Versus the Nugget

Last night as I lay here, I was thinking of the comparisons in values; for example, that between a large cinder and a gold nugget. It seems impossible to imagine that the finding of a cinder could create as much feeling of excitement as would a gold nugget.

I was sitting on the tip behind the tram sheds at East Jarrow. It was the residue of fires from forgotten years. It was still quite large although it had been riddled over by countless men in their search for half-burnt cinders or some minute scraps of coal to be used on a fire so that the wife could make a baking for the family; perhaps there would even be enough to fill a barrow, and which might, with luck, be sold for a shilling. This was the time of not only a strike but also a slump, and some might not have been in work for years.

But there was I, this particular morning, sitting on the tip raking away, with, as yet, not more than half a dozen cinders in the bottom of my bag. There was no-one from whom Kate could have borrowed a bucket of coal and she had the idea of making little cakes to sell with ginger beer. Things were tight in the house and, as always when this happened, I was happy. She might make enough for a pint or so, but that didn't worry me as long as there was no hard stuff.

So, in order to get the oven going, I had come on the tip. She hadn't asked me, but she hadn't stopped me. And there was me granda. All he had to do was to see to his hens in the backyard and now and again take them for a walk down the field flanking the terrace. This was when they needed medicine, which they got from grass, and a bit of grit, which hardened their shells. And it was a sight indeed to see those hens and the two ducks walking behind him as if in formation. Having only this to do, why didn't he get himself to the tip and pick cinders?

Oh no. That would be very lowering; he couldn't do that. But what he would do, after an hour or so, on such an occasion, was walk towards the tram sheds and carry the sack, which was never very full, home for me.

This time when there was about a bucketful of cinders in the sack, and not one of them larger than a walnut, I was about to give up when I stuck my rake in for the last time and, behold! it caught at something, and when I pulled it upwards my astonished and delighted gaze was looking down on a huge cinder. Well, it wasn't really a cinder, it was more than half coal that hadn't been burnt through. It was as large as a turnip and I weighed it in my two hands as a gold prospector way out in what they call the Klondike would have done if he had unearthed a gold nugget.

I recall holding it up and looking towards two men raking at the far end of the heap, but they were too intent on what they were doing to take any notice of a bit lass in the same boat as themselves, so I placed my gold nugget carefully in the sack; then began to rake madly around where it had lain in an endeavour to find others of the same size. I did not, but the result of the excited raking was a half-filled sack of decent cinders, and I realised that the man who had cleaned out that fire hadn't done his job properly, or all those good cinders wouldn't have been thrown away but would have been the basis for the next fire.

From this distance, I could compare my discovery of the large cinder with that of the gold nugget held by the prospector, and at that moment my joy at my find must have equalled his; and moreover, I knew that mine bred hopes of future gains along such lines, whereas his, like many another under the same circumstances, would end up as spent as the cinders on the tip.

What is Love?

Love is caring, understanding, putting up with
   foibles;
Love is listening when the desire in you is to talk;
Love is defending in right and still defending in
   wrong;
Love is recognising a good point and enlarging on
   it;
Love is boosting someone's small ego;
Love for another is knowing yourself first, and
   knowing when verbally to hit out and bring to
   the surface needed retaliation;
Love is bringing light to another when his sky is
   overcast;
Love is all the things you find most difficult to do
   for someone you don't like;
Love is that spark of ecstasy that cannot be held;
It is not the demand for satisfaction in bed, nor the
   patient submission that breeds disgust;
Love has nothing to do with the fantasies of the
   night;
Love is a battle between self will, self desire, self
   pity, greed and pride . . .
Love is pain.

20 June 1990

(Entry from my diary on my eighty-fourth birthday)

It doesn't seem to matter:

Time is swift, and Time is all.
How little we have of it;
And at the end,
None at all:
We need not have been,
We need not have come:
Nothing from nothing,
We subtract the sum.

I am low today.
Come on – come on, woman!
Smile, at least for Tom;
Be thankful you've got this far;
Look at all the gifts,
Acts of love
From all quarters.
Really, you know,
You should be grateful.

A Plea

Lord, if Thou be, go easy with me when we
    meet,
And don't censure me for not grovelling at
    Your feet;
For remember, You gave me a mind to use,
To think, to reason, and with which to muse;
So why provide me with this apparatus at all?
Surely, not to fear You
Or believe in Adam's fall.
That is not what a mind is for;
At least to my way of thinking.
No; it is to use thought
On people, sights, and sounds, and touch.
By this and such
Comes the means of understanding Your
    creation
And why I'm here on earth at all.
I can't think I'm wrong in my reasoning,
For I've pondered so much;
But if I am off the mark, have a heart,
For as you know, I had a tough start:
Number 10 was no country seat.
So, Lord, go easy with me when we meet.

Peace

So much has been written about that elusive quality, peace of mind and of spirit, but I don't think one can achieve the former without the latter, and in my case, the search has taken up more than half my life.

Before I had my breakdown in 1945, I didn't really know for what I was searching. I thought my troubles had mainly been caused by the stigma of illegitimacy and of having been brought up with drink and, as I grew older, the constant feeling of illness due to my inherited vascular trouble, which kept me in a state of constant anaemia, but which had been assumed by doctors to be the result of my temperament, for was I not working, 'like nobody else', fourteen hours a day?

The climax came when I threw off God. That, in the ordinary way, one would think, would wreck my chances of ever coming to terms with peace of mind and spirit. But, no, it didn't; what it did was, it forced me to go to school again, and this was a rough place with only two teachers, reason and history, both of whom were opposed by an outside one, whom I would not accept, called faith.

The second teacher I found difficult because recorded history went back a few thousand years and touched on many civilisations, each worshipping its own Gods or God, some, surprisingly, with virgin mothers, which became an added stumbling block.

Nevertheless, my mind attended this school for many years, over thirty, in fact, and I was anything but a brilliant scholar. However, I did learn something: If you are happy in your choice of a God, stick with Him. He may be only a screen against fear, or a prop to help you through this mystery called life, but this is better than being thrust into the wilderness where all is night and there is no hand to guide you.

As to reason, I brought this down to love, or up, whichever way one prefers to place it. At least it brings one a modicum of peace. With me, it came about by reverting back to a habit I had almost lost: If you love, speak of it, speak it out, for she or he will not be able to hear you from the grave. It may be hard for many of us to give as a daily medicine those three words 'I love you'; but how much better both the patients and you will feel.

Lastly, it was forced on to me to accept that you come into this world without owning anything but yourself, and that's the way you go out. You can't take anything with you, money, property, belongings.

That was difficult at first for me to accept, for I've collected bits and pieces over the last sixty years. Yet I've had to look at it this way: nearly every piece I have in my house was once owned by someone else, and, after I die, will again be owned by someone else. I came to realise that the only thing I possessed and could really call my own was my soul, or spirit, and that I could take with me; and from it the still small

34

voice said: You seek peace, so, be kind, in word and deed be kind . . . give, give while you can, and all you can.

The third teacher, faith, still eludes me.

My First Novel

(*Published in* The Author *some years ago*)

I scribbled, first, when I was eleven years old; I scribbled during my teens, and on and off during my twenties; but I did not WRITE until I was forty and in a breakdown, which had been contributed to by my having been aware for thirty-three of those forty years that I was a bastard. It was this same knowledge which, eventually, caused me to flee my early environment and to build up a thick façade around all I had left behind. However, later, I was to make the mistake of bringing my past, which centred around my parent, from three hundred and fifty miles away into my new life, and my façade was penetrated.

What I soon realised was that I was an upstart playing at being a lady *à la* Lord Chesterfield who, when I was twenty, had become my tutor through his *Letters To His Son*, and that I could give up all idea of ever writing anything that anyone would want to read until I faced up to the fact of what I actually was, a self-educated illegitimate with no real knowledge of the world except that which had been ground into me during my childhood. I also faced up to the fact that it had taken a long time for me to get into this breakdown and it was going to take a long time to get out of it.

So what was I going to do about it?

Well, now began the writing career.

Having walked out, after a six weeks' voluntary stay in the mental hospital outside Hereford, all I wanted to do was to get back to my home in Hastings which I had left in 1940, a month after we were married, and now it was June 1945.

In my mind, at that time, there was no thought of writing: what I wanted to do was to put this 'gentleman's residence' back in order after its five years' neglect and the ravishes of bomb damage, which was a daunting task. So, between vomiting with fear against the terrible aggressiveness that might lead me to do something dreadful, I worked fourteen to sixteen hours a day inside and outside that very large house, and alone, for Tom was still in the Air Force. In fact, looking back, I feel now that I was consumed with fear throughout the whole twenty-four hours, for I never seemed to sleep, just doze. In a bout of bravado I had thrown all my 'quieting pills' down the lavatory.

If a breakdown does any good at all it is when it holds a mirror up to the self. I was devastated by the thought that I had nerves. Only lazy people had nerves. As Kate had said: anything you've got wrong with you can be worked off. And that had been my motto: work it off. Mentally or physically, work it off. But work as I would and did, I was overcome with the deep shame of having succumbed to nerves, for who would ever associate

Kitty with nerves! The life and soul of the party; the business woman; the artist; and hadn't she written three plays, short stories by the dozen, poems . . . NERVES! Nerves were shameful. I wouldn't have minded being lumbered with a crippling disease, but nerves!

For years I had been petrified that people would get to know about my early beginnings and birth and Kate's drinking. Now here was another matter for petrification: they would say I had been in an asylum; in fact, they did say this. But I was a very good hand at façades. Moreover – remember the time – I was a grammar-schoolmaster's wife, with a part to play. And I played that part even though, underneath, I was going through hell. As it is the clown's, so laughter was my defence, in my case hiding a desperate person living a private life in an abyss of fear and hate which all the time caused me to crave retribution on those, or on one in particular, who had brought me to this state. What could I do about it?

The answer came: WRITE IT OUT.

Write about what you know, about the background in which Kate and your granny had been brought up. Forget about Chesterfield and lords and ladies and their big houses. Get rid of them. Face up to the fact of your early beginnings; think of the people you knew in the New Buildings, and those in Tyne Dock and Jarrow and South Shields, weave a story around them. Bring in Kate as you know she could have been, and that will sublimate this terrible feeling that you have against her. Go on, get down to it! It's your only hope.

So my first real story was born.

I had never attempted a novel before. How did one go about it? Well, if I was going to write about the past, I must first set it in an environment.

Environment. That word has remained the lodestar in my type of writing. Environment. Get that, place people in it, and their reactions to it will give you the story.

Well, right from the word go I knew that my environment in *Kate Hannigan*, as I called the story, was right. Of course, it had to have an illegitimate child in it, and its mother had to be an intelligent woman. Our Kate was intelligent, in her own way; but the character of Kate Hannigan in the book had to be larger than life: she had to be as I hoped our Kate would have been; and, of course, she had to fall in love with someone out of her class.

The main thing, however, was, I had a background, and from such a background I had the reactions, the real reactions of people I had known: the meanness, the kindness, the love, the hate, the ignorance and superstition of the poor which cannot really be described unless you have lived amongst it. And not only the poor, the upper working class, the breeding ground of snobbery.

Writing that first chapter, I seemed to come into my own. I ended it on a cliffhanger. I did the same with the second and the third chapters. I made the events of each chapter take place on a Christmas Eve. I thought this very clever. It was later scrapped.

During this time I had joined the new Writers' Circle in Hastings. It didn't do me very much good, except it gave me a platform from which to read my

Mary Ann stories, which formed the series of eight novels about her. I later became secretary.

On looking back, I recall some very good writers in that small group and that most of the members seemed to be getting bits and pieces published in magazines or newspapers.

But I was writing my novel.

It was during the winter of 1948 that the library issued a notice stating that a talk would be given on how to write a novel by that eminent author Major Christopher Bush.

It was on the wildest of nights when I ventured out – I had to be helped across the deserted square by a policeman – and when I reached the upper room of the library, there, present, were about twelve old girls. At the time, I was only forty-two!

The major's talk angered me, for he repeatedly stated that anyone who could write a laundry list could write a novel.

When that gentleman sat down I stood up and dared to contradict him. I, I said, in my fourteen and a half years working in a laundry, ten as manageress, had written thousands of laundry lists, but they hadn't helped me to write a novel. I recall the amazed silence from the audience.

Afterwards, standing outside in the storm, I thought, Eeh! fancy saying that to *that man*. And having realised that I had once again marched in where angels feared to tread, I returned to the room and apologised.

And that gentleman not only accepted my apology with a smile but said I had been perfectly right and that it was a silly thing to say, and that he had said it countless times when talking to ladies; but never again.

Had I an agent? he then asked me.

An agent? No; I hadn't an agent. Agents hadn't been touched upon in the Writers' Circle; in fact, I had the impression they were a species who should be avoided.

'How much of your novel have you written?'

'Three chapters.'

'Then send it to my agent' he said; 'Christy & Moore. They'll give you an opinion on it.'

'Thank you. Thank you.' What a nice man. Yes, I would do that right away, I told him.

And that's what I did; and received a reply back in a very short time from one John Smith who said, 'As soon as you get this story finished let me have it.' I didn't know then that this man was to be my lifelong friend and that he, too, had just entered the business.

Inspired now, I worked on that story every minute I could. At the same time I imagined I was ridding myself of this dreadful breakdown, of the fears and aggression, and the self-pity. One thing I was doing, I was hitting back at the Catholic Church, because its doctrine had brought fear of the devil and hell into my existence. However, always trying to be fair, in the story I brought in two priests who expressed the good and the bad in the Catholic doctrine; and in the last chapter I went to town in a summing up of my feelings about them, all woven around, of course, the hero and the heroine.

It took me a year to complete that story; then it was off to John Smith. From him, it went to

MacDonald & Company, Publishers, to one Murray Thompson, the head of the firm, who read the first three pages, then threw it to his secretary, saying, 'Get rid of that! It's too grim.' She, dear soul, looked at those three pages, took the book home, sat up half the night reading it, came back the next morning and said to him, 'I think you've missed something here.' The result was, it was sent to a reader, a Mr Malcolm Elwin who, I came to understand, was an exponent of written English. In his report he said, 'I don't know how old this writer is, but if she is young she will go somewhere.' I was then forty-three years old. Another thing he said: 'I would recommend this book be accepted if the writer rewrites the last chapter.'

As I have intimated, in the last chapter I had given the patient, the reader, the whole bottle of medicine against Catholicism, instead of a spoonful. And so I followed Mr Elwin's advice; and I was away.

What is it like to have your first novel published? Only those who have undergone this ego-inflation can hope to understand. You have written a book; it is going to be published. You are an author. AN AUTHOR. You are on top of the world; it is there kneeling at your feet.

But what had it done for my breakdown? Had it rid me of all the fear, the night terrors, the dreadful aggressiveness that lay behind the façade? No; these were all still there, and, unfortunately, were to remain there until my mother died in 1956 and I started to write my autobiography. It was from this time things began to ease; but slowly, for that book was to cover twelve years in its making.

And then there was the invitation to have lunch with the publisher . . . my publisher! What an honour!

Dressed in my best, I sat in the early bus to the station amidst work-weary and husband-weary women, and longed to say, 'I am Catherine Cookson the writer. I have had my first book published. I'm on my way to London to have lunch with my publisher.' Had I done so, the reaction would have been, 'So what!'

In the train, I sat opposite an old gentleman who sniffed all the way to Victoria; and I even chatted to him. And I wouldn't have been surprised to have been met at the station by the Mayor and Corporation.

Having been directed across a road to get a bus, I happened to step in front of a taxi whose bad braking then caused a lorry to come to a premature stop. I was amazed at the language. Of course, they didn't know I was Catherine Cookson the author in London to have lunch with her publisher.

MacDonald's offices in Maddox Street were a disappointment. I was eventually shown up the narrow staircase to the sanctum sanctorum, there to be met by a very surprised man.

I had come on the wrong day!

So much for my first novel.

I had written eighteen by the time my autobiography was published. It had been a long 'spring cleaning', and I sat back and waited for congratulations from my friends.

Two sisters phoned. 'Dear Kitty,' they said, 'we have read your life story. But oh dear me! we think you have made a big mistake; you have completely lost your image; you have done yourself so much damage, because you see, dear, before, you could have been taken for a lady!'

Well! Well!

Getting What You Want

I had always wanted to live graciously, but at twenty-seven, still unmarried and no rich man in sight who was to carry out my plan, I came across The Hurst, Hoadswood Road, Hastings.

I was earning a very large wage then, for a woman, of £3 a week plus six shillings in lieu of my dinners in the workhouse. I lived, more or less, on this six shillings, perhaps I should have said I almost starved on it, and moved my digs in order to save further, ending up in a garret at eight shillings and sixpence a week, and so was able to increase my endowment with the Sun Life of Canada to £750. It was this which enabled me to take out a mortgage on the 'Gentleman's Residence'. It was two miles from the town centre, and stood in what, to me at that time, was a large garden.

Stupidly, because she beseeched me that she, too, wanted a different life, and swore she was practically teetotal, I had brought my mother from the North to live with me in my flat; and I have to admit that the purchasing of The Hurst was then prompted as much by the aim to get her away from the bars in the old town as to have a beautiful house to myself – by this time I should have known that the word of an alcoholic cannot be trusted – and in doing so I was to suffer two more years of the hell and shame I thought I had left behind me for ever when I left the North.

The house had indeed been a gentleman's residence. But I knew nothing about buying a house. How could I? So when I saw the new floor going down in the large drawing room I thought, How marvellous, a new floor.

When I saw the new sewer going in at the bottom of the garden I wondered about it, and I told myself how lucky I was to have a new sewer. The tree roots had grown through the old one. It took ten more years for the tree roots to go through the new one, but nevertheless they did so.

Then there was the butler's pantry.

The estate agent was an absolute expert at his job. He had studied human nature. He knew all about hidden desires, especially those of upstarts, so he kept on plugging the butler's pantry and its adjacent little wine-cellar. Again may I say, this was happening in 1933.

How could Katie McMullen from 10 William Black Street resist a butler's pantry, I ask you?

The house had a lovely hall with a long stained-glass window at one end, and the walls were half panelled in ornamental wooden squares. But how was I to know they were riddled with woodworm?

Afterwards I did think it was a pity that when the men were replacing the rotten floor in the drawing room, they hadn't also renewed the two-foot skirting board that ran all round it. This was the morning when the hoover went through it, so showing the source of the odd smell.

Then there was the roof. Oh, the roof! Well,

during the first storm, I mean real storm, for we'd had no evidence of what was wrong from just a shower, the landing floor became almost awash! As time went on, so the number of utensils to catch the water increased until we ran out of jugs and basins.

And yet, from the outside the roof looked so attractive, seeming to be criss-crossed, Italian style, with little gullies.

Yet I loved that house. It was the outcome of a dream; but then everything you want in this life has to be paid for and it saw to it that I paid dearly. Only one good thing came out of it: when my mother and I parted, she was out to show me what she could do; and so she took a large house to enable her to take guests.

When, in 1937 the drink again beat her and she returned to the North, her one remaining guest came to live at The Hurst. His name was Thomas Henry Cookson.

How to Die

For some months during late 1988, I kept in touch over the phone with a friend who was dying of cancer. Her name was Beryl Cotterell. She was aware that she was dying and that there was no hope of reprieve; but not I, and so it was not at first discussed. At times, her cheerfulness and thoughtfulness put me to shame. I myself was ill yet, like the creaking door that I am, I knew that my hinges would last for some time; but there she was, getting weaker and weaker every day, often having to be lifted from the bed to the window from where she could look out on to pasture land, which she loved.

I had sent her my book *Let Me Make Myself Plain*, and a couple of days later her husband Laurence phoned me to say that they'd had the dire news that nothing more could be done for her. At this I actually cried at him, 'Oh, my goodness! You haven't got that book yet, have you? She mustn't see it because I am dealing quite a bit with death, at least my idea of it.'

In answer, he said, 'She's got it and she's read it and I've never known her to be so impressed with anything, and so happy.'

'Really?'

'Yes, really. I'll put her on.'

What Beryl said was, 'Oh, Catherine, you've got no idea what your writings have done for me this day.'

It was the greatest compliment that I'll ever have with regard to *Let Me Make Myself Plain*. I recall she went on to discuss my essays. Apparently we thought along the same lines concerning our earthly demise and future.

Following this our almost daily chats were about the book and were interspersed with much laughter. There was a time when I told her I had written to Mr Ray Branch at The Healing Sanctuary and that he and all there were praying for her. It was the next day she said to me, 'I feel so free, you've got no idea. I know they are sticking drugs into me, but this feeling is different, it's a kind of peace.'

Then came the day when her voice was a little thick and blurred, which pointed to the nearing of her time. At this end of the phone I was in a flood of tears, for she was thanking me for what *Let Me Make Myself Plain* had done for her.

There again was the book which I had hated compiling and considered of little value.

She had been looked after by Laurence, a woman friend, and her sons, and so I knew that everything possible was being done for her.

But how was she dying?

It was Christmas Eve when Laurence phoned me. She was going so peacefully, he said, and she had spoken of me and was sending me a gift.

I received the gift later. It was a book entitled

The Prophet by Kahlil Gibran, and inside were the words.

> To much-loved Catherine from Beryl
> who treasured this little volume.
> In memoriam. Christmas Eve 1988.

She died that night.
Her book is full of wisdom, but it is Beryl who has taught me how to die.

Memories

KINDNESS LINGERS AND FADES, BUT INSULTS
REMAIN FOR EVER.

'This is my wife Kitty,' said Tom.

The schoolmaster looked me straight in the face
and in a high-falutin' voice said, 'Can you tell me
where I'll get my shirts washed?'

We had been evacuated with the school to St
Albans. We had been there a fortnight and we had
only recently been married.

The master's name was Ryan. I've never forgotten
him.

My reception into the scholastic world had been
friendly; but I was no fool, I was suspect in many
quarters. Well, I ask you: a girl, or young woman,
who had worked in a laundry since she was eighteen
and at twenty-seven had bought a 'Gentleman's
Residence' in the country, and with no visible man
behind her. And look at all the odd people she
boarded in this new house, a mental girl, an
epileptic, two TB patients, and an army captain, who
also had a name for he earned his free drink by
standing in the bar of a well-known hotel every
evening: he was a gentleman, a charming one, who
could attract company. And although she ran her
house as a guest-house she still managed the

workhouse laundry. And then, of course, there was her mother, back in the North now, a woman who drank like a fish, a common woman.

It was all very strange; and the strangest thing was she had now married young Tom Cookson and she six years older than him, he such a quiet little fellow and she an extrovert of extroverts.

Oh, I knew I had a name, and the unfairness of it had often caused me to cry at nights for I was a reluctant virgin. I was warm-hearted, and wanting love, but determined, however hungry I was for it, not to go the way of my mother.

Before I was married in 1940 I had met only four single men since arriving in Hastings. One would have married me had I been a nurse, for he had ideas of starting up a home for elderly gentlemen who needed nursing. The second one was surprising. He was the insurance agent whom the company sent to see me when I put up my insurance. I did this as a result of living in a garret in order to save another few shillings a week.

Imagine my amazement when the said young man's parents came to see me and begged me to let him go, as he was almost engaged to a girl and friend of the family. I sent them away happy.

Funny about that insurance. A 'lien' was added to the policy, for I was illegitimate! Moreover, each time I wished to raise the insurance I had to see my doctor. At that time he was Doctor Nesbit Wood of Hastings. I recall him looking at me hard and asking, 'What are you doing this for, a young woman like you? You thinking of committing suicide?'

So I explained to him – which astonished him

further – by saying I was saving through an endowment to provide me with the things I would never be given by anyone else, as I didn't expect to marry – the single ones weren't queuing up. In any case I would never marry just for marrying's sake, if he followed me.

He did.

And then there was another doctor who had his doubts about me. I had left the workhouse laundry just before the war started, and during the first year of it I took in twelve male blind evacuees from the East End of London. I have written about this elsewhere. One of them took ill and the doctor from the workhouse was called in. We knew each other, of course; and I wasn't then married.

We were coming down the stairs when he suddenly stopped and looked about him and, in awed tones, he said, 'Do you really own this house, Miss McMullen?'

'Yes, I do,' I said.

There was a pause before he muttered, 'But how on earth did you manage to buy it?'

I looked him straight in the eye and answered, 'Well, what would you expect, Doctor? Before the war I used to take weekend trips to London and Paris – very select.' Red-faced, he hurried away.

When, a month later, he had to examine me for internal bleeding, I wondered if he would become more red-faced still when he discovered there was definitely one way I had not earned the money to buy my house.

I used to get so angry about this. Yet when I look back I now see myself as someone before her time.

How many single young women were there in their twenties who would 'take out' an insurance policy which would stand as security for a house, not any old house but a 'Gentleman's Residence'? Yes; yes, I admit there was the unknown gentleman father as a spur, and snobbery too.

The third single man did what in those days was called 'jilted me'. He was very nice but couldn't understand my reluctance to jump the marriage licence. He wrote me a letter in which he said women like me should be hanged. I was living in a garret, and I cried half the night whilst asking myself if virginity was worth the candle. Then I started to bleed, to wake up, in the morning, everything about me stiff with blood.

Again I asked myself what was wrong with me. Was it because I was illegitimate, and had I inherited something that attracted the wrong types, for there had been more than one gentleman who had suddenly discovered he had married the wrong woman, when my reaction had been to pick up my skirts and run from the word divorce.

Then I found something in me that was right, for when my Tom first set eyes on me he came to me like a bee to honey. And although our three years' courtship was as rough going as anything I'd ever been through before – my mother, with the weakness of the alcoholic, being an inveterate liar, aided and abetted by a so-called friend, sorely tried our love to the limit – we were fortified by the knowledge that we were made for each other, which had been proved by our living in my house for three years as friends, and in those days the word friend meant just what it says.

We were married, and I entered the scholastic world and met Mr Ryan, only to find out there were female Ryans too. Yet they're all dead now, and, strangely, I'm left.

I hope Mr Ryan gets his shirts washed, wherever he is.

The Mink Coat

I sat before the tax man. He was a new fellow, young. His predecessor had been such a nice man, a real human being, and nobody thinks of a tax man as a human being; but I remember he wrote me a funny letter once. It was actually about the fact that I'd been overcharged in some way, and he finished by saying, 'Don't ever give up writing, Mrs Cookson, else I'll be out of a job.'

But this one sitting staring at me was a different kettle of fish and, what was more, he had been educated at the Grammar School.

Anyway he required my presence to let me know that he was not going to allow me to claim tax relief on a £500 set of the *Encyclopaedia Britannica*, bought to help me with my work.

Owing to my blood complaint, I was restricted in my travelling, so even though I couldn't describe people and places from personal experience, I could read about them in this excellent work.

The new, young, and I can say raw, tax man did not see it this way. I could get books from the library; well, in my position I could buy them.

At this stage I pointed out I was always buying books, and that this encyclopaedia was another example, but, in this case, its cost of £500 would then, to me, have been prohibitive and I wouldn't have afforded it unless I thought I would be able to claim it in my tax expenses.

I was utterly amazed when he came back, saying, 'You couldn't afford it, yet you're wearing a mink coat. You could afford that.'

I couldn't believe my ears at the nerve of this young man: not only was he ill-mannered, but he certainly, as yet, did not know his job, that was, how to deal with people. I am sure that in their training would-be tax collectors are instructed not to make personal remarks about whomever they might be interviewing.

I recall standing up and saying, 'It's none of your business what I'm wearing; but I'll tell you this: I never bought this mink coat, it was given to me. Understand? It was given to me.'

I can see him sitting there, his lips tight, his eyes looking straight at me as he said, 'Oh yes,' almost as a question, to which I reacted with, 'I am not going to take your word for this, sir, I am going to see my accountant and get him to take it to a tribunal. Good day to you.'

After relating all this to Tom, I asked, 'Did you ever hear anything like that, and from a tax man? Did you know him at school? Do you remember him?'

He shook his head. 'Not really. Vaguely. I just vaguely remember him. I don't think I took him in at all.'

'Well whether you did or not, he's got it in for me. He hated the sight of me from the beginning. Why? And just think how Mr So-and-So used to treat one.

Someone wants to take him out of that chair and retrain him. Talk about tax men getting a bad name; no wonder, if they're all like him. But then we know they're not. We've never had any trouble before.'

We next saw Bill, my accountant. He couldn't believe that I was not to be allowed to charge the encyclopaedia on my expenses; and straightaway he said, 'I'll take this to a tribunal.'

He took it. A tribunal, I understand, is made up of a number of professional or business men practising in the area, who go thoroughly into the complainant's business and report back to the local Chief Inspector of Taxes.

The phone rang. It was Bill and from the sound of his voice I could imagine he was grinning from ear to ear. Apparently, in my case, the members had first looked at my income, then at my expenses, and without any confab had agreed with one word: Ridiculous. Evidently, they were amazed at the smallness of my expenses compared with my income.

Later on, I think I might have discovered this particular tax man's animosity towards me. It was from hearing a friend, who had had an up and downer with him, say, 'He has a chip on his shoulder, and he's an utter snob. Likely, because his father just drives a van and delivers for So-and-So, you know, the grocer.'

Well so and so the grocer we had dealt with for years, and I'd found the man who usually delivered the groceries to be a very nice man, a very nice man indeed.

From when he was still at school, this young man

must have known his father delivered to Mr Cookson's wife, which would have imbued in him, as it would in many young people in those days, a certain pride in his father, only for this to disappear when he left school and began to climb the social ladder.

In those days I wasn't earning what, today, would be called big money, but I suppose my income was quite something compared with that of other professions. Yet I would never, at that time, have been able to buy a mink coat, and I had spoken the truth when I said it was given to me.

It really had been given to me, and it had come about in this way.

Some years earlier I was needing a part-time typist. The one who had been doing my work was getting married and going off abroad. I hadn't advertised, but one morning there was a telephone call and a quiet refined voice said, 'I hear you are needing a typist. I've had experience as a court stenographer for some years; I would like to apply for the position.'

I explained to her it wasn't all that much of a position, that I was a novelist and what I wanted was someone who would come for an hour or two when I needed her.

Well, said the caller, she'd be very thankful if I'd give her the opportunity to take on the work.

And that's how it started.

She was a good-looking woman in her thirties, tall and rather delicate, and she told me she had been in this country only a short time. She had brought her two daughters here to be educated, and to this end she had rented a small bungalow in Fairlight, which was all of five miles from Hastings.

This information was rather puzzling to me. Here was this educated woman having her daughters educated in England, yet glad to take on this meagre post, for which I wasn't offering any brilliant wage. At that time I couldn't have afforded it. Another thing: she seemed so happy in her work, and she always enjoyed the cup of hot coffee and toast waiting for her, because her journey to us would have taken more than half an hour.

We worked together very amicably. I only had to get on the phone and she would drop everything she was doing and come over, perhaps for only a couple of hours' work. She wasn't forthcoming about why she was really in England alone with her daughters, nor did I probe, until one morning I looked out of the window and saw coming down the drive the most magnificent figure. It was this tall and beautiful woman in the most exquisite fur coat.

I greeted her with, 'Oh, you do look lovely. And what a beautiful coat, magnificent! It's just like the Queen's.' It had similar wide sleeves and high collar.

It was on this morning that she told me why she was in England but that unfortunately she'd soon have to leave, to go to Australia where her husband was now living with his Chinese mistress from Hong Kong. What was more, he had sent her the tickets for the passage for the three of them, but not a penny extra; and besides the children needing outfits there would be money needed for travelling and the accessories necessary for the journey. It was for this she was wearing the fur coat: on leaving me she would be going straight on to London to visit her friends to see if any of them would buy it. I was surprised, amazed and appalled by what she was telling me, the while wondering how she had existed, being so penniless. I heard myself asking how on earth she had managed when the children came home from school for their holidays, and her replying briefly, 'With difficulty.'

I was saddened to the heart for her, a lovely woman like her to be in such a fix, and as, later, I said goodbye to her I asked her to let me know how she got on in London.

It was around nine o'clock the same evening when the phone rang. She hadn't been able to sell her coat, she reported sadly: all her friends loved it, but none of them had enough money to buy it. I gauged that most of them must live hand to mouth in order to keep up appearances. She did not sound bitter, only sad. But then, tentatively, she asked if I would buy it. She just needed a few pounds to get them ready for the voyage. Once she was in Australia she felt sure she could and would get good employment.

My answer to her was immediate because Tom and I had talked it over during the day. No, I wouldn't buy her coat because that was one of the things she would need on her journey, by boat, but I would loan her whatever she needed, and she needn't hurry about paying it back.

Her answer was: if she were to accept the money I must take the coat, to which my reply was: no, certainly not; I didn't want her coat. As much as I would have loved it, I was in no way going to deprive her of that beautiful garment.

'Oh, Mrs Cookson. Oh, Mrs Cookson,' was her only response.

I told her to pop in in the morning, when the cheque would be ready for her because we were going off to our little boat berthed in Cambridge. Tom had started his holidays and we'd likely be away two weeks. That was a wishful arrangement, because very rarely did we stay a week: we would no sooner get there than he would want to come back; there was the garden to see to and there would likely be some boy who needed help. So on and so on.

Anyway, the next morning she arrived with the coat parcelled up; but she left with it again, together with a cheque that would see to all her needs until she arrived in Australia.

Later in the day, we ourselves left the house, together with the dog, our dear Bill, and numerous cases and bags ready for our sojourn on the water. At that time we did not have a car, and so the journey from Hastings to Cambridge was fraught with problems, for Bill hated the trains and was petrified of escalators. Anyway, dogs weren't allowed actually on escalators, so Tom would have to carry him, and Bill was of no small weight.

True to pattern we were back home within a week, and our next-door neighbour brought in a package that had come for me two days after we left.

I opened it, and there was the fur coat.

Although I put it on and knew I loved it, I was having none of it, oh no. Anyway, it had likely cost six times what I had loaned her. So what did I do but parcel it up again and send it back to her at the Australian address she had given me.

It must have been four months later when the parcel was at my door again and a letter inside, saying, 'If you send it back I shall only return it again. I want you to have it. I have been offered a good position. Everything will be all right. I shall never forget your kindness to me.' A PS to the letter stated: 'I am applying for a divorce.'

So I had a fur coat, this beautiful, beautiful fur coat.

A further three months and I received another letter with a cheque in it for the amount I had loaned her: the coat was her gift to me and she was so happy that I had it. But I couldn't get over the fact that it was mine.

Of course, it was so posh that I could wear it only on occasions, but wear it I did. This again raised eyebrows: by! I must be making a pile out of those books; and after all, what were they? just stories of common working people being badly treated, and generally by the middle class of the times.

But what about the tax man? He would never have believed this story. Surely, no-one of his type would have ever given away as much as a rabbit skin, never mind a mink coat.

He was the fly in the ointment of all the tax men I've had to deal with for, both before and afterwards, I found them fair and understanding, right from the first one I went to and from whom I had received a tax demand for £2.10s.

The tax office was situated in a lovely house

opposite the indoor swimming pool in Hastings. I recall my indignation as I faced this first and rather small man: What did they mean I had to pay £2.10s. I had received only £100 for my book, and look what I had to pay out of it!

Yes; but I had a husband who was a schoolmaster and I was now an author; I'm afraid, my dear, you are due to pay tax.

Deflated, I said, 'What am I going to do about it?'

He could simply have told me to pay up and look pleasant, but what he did was advise me in a quiet voice to get an accountant to see to my affairs.

'I am not supposed to do this,' he confided so nicely, 'but I would recommend to you a young man, Mr William McBrien. He is in the offices of Gibbons and Mitchell in Wellington Square, and he is a very honest and kind young man, I can assure you. You will do well to put your business in his hands.'

I thanked him very warmly.

Out in the street I thought, what a nice man! and he a tax man; and all the things they say about tax men!

I found Mr William McBrien to be a rather shy young man and that day he was indeed very kind, and I felt assured that he would also be very honest. Today, forty-eight years later, he is still kind and very honest and my very good friend. He is only troubled by the fact that he has hardly any expenses to place before the tax man. He has never been able to say I was travelling to Timbuctoo to get material for my new book and for which my expenses were so and so; nor has he been able to put down an enormous dress allowance because, although I bought my clothes second-hand and paid more for some of them than I would have done if I had bought new ones, my expenses in that direction compared to my income and my appearance on this or that platform or show were almost negligible.

Moreover, I did not give literary parties or a big do whenever a book came out.

What was more, I had a very honest agent, a very honest publisher, and now a very, very honest accountant and, what was more and worse, a husband who had a phobia to tell the truth.

How can a poor woman hope to do the tax man, when set against that moral quartet!

Within Walls

All life is lived within walls
Of flesh, of brick, of wood, of wattle,
Of wattle, or wood, or brick, or flesh;
Only the soul escapes the entangling mesh
And, above clouds of thought where time is the
    moment
And naught can be bought or sold or swapped or
    borrowed or lent,
Where life is for ever and yet already spent,
Draws from the laws of boundless space
Substance to face Life encased within walls
Of flesh, or brick, or wood, or wattle.

The Payment

My first novels were reviewed in *The Times Lit Sup* and *The Sunday Times*. These books were, to my mind, social histories of the North-east covering my mother's and my grandmother's times.

I think there's a middle period in all writers' lives: the press gives them a line or two when they are new to the game; then comes that long desert when it would seem that, for all the critics know, you could have been found dead in it, except that, in the meantime, the public have kept you supplied with the water of life which, to a writer, means that they are reading you.

This goes on until the day the magic words 'a million sales' are heard, and WHAM! you're resurrected, and it's quantity now not quality in which they are interested.

For my part I've never written for money. I once astonished my agent, in fact he nearly fell on the floor, when I asked him not to press my publisher for a rise on my next book, that I was quite satisfied with what I was getting: we had enough to live on . . . our needs were simple. He thought I was clean barmy; no author talked like that. That was twelve years ago.

If one is wise, and how many of us are? one should be content with a good living. But then people get greedy; and that's when the trouble starts.

I was advised some years ago, for tax purposes, to go and live in Jersey. So, with my little entourage I booked up for four days on that island, and within four hours of arriving I'd been introduced to the big house I could buy and the gentlemen who were going to take me over.

Well, I'm an individualist and the idea of being taken over by anyone, let alone by gentlemen who were going to control my earnings and treble them by investing in some strange-sounding foreign country, and stated flatly that I must get rid of my agent, didn't appeal to me, although the deal promised that I'd likely have my own aeroplane in no time. But with all such wonderful deals there was a snag, in fact, more than one. First I'd have to leave England, but I'd be allowed back a few months a year. Funny, but up till then I had never thought about my feeling for England; but the result of it actually took place the very next morning when, at seven o'clock, I phoned my husband and said that I couldn't live in Jersey, even if the Labour Government took not only the 83 pence in every pound I earned, but 99 pence.

Those few days on that island made me realise I couldn't live anywhere but in England. All right, I resented having to pay her not only the 83 pence in the pound, but her taking all the interest except 2 pence in the pound of my hard-earned savings which had started as a child in that far-off lavatory where I hid my little store of pennies.

You would have thought that having been brought up on the dock front, as it were, of Tyneside, and having seen little else for twenty-two years but docks, shipyards, steel works and greasy streets, I would have plumped for Jersey, followed by Switzerland, Barbados, or the Costa Brava, but no, like an idiot I plumped to work twelve or fourteen hours a day to pay for last year's tax. But when all's said and done, and that takes in our present situation, I don't think there can be a better place to live, a freer place to live than in this country. And as in life everything one has must be paid for in one way or another, I was paying dearly.

After all I've said in my autobiography about my early beginnings, I can say I am glad I was born when I was, slump, poverty, grime included, because my whole life has been an education in values, and without the resulting trauma I know I wouldn't have been capable of assessing them and the positive side to their negation.

Even at this late stage of my life one absolute fact remains, we all need money in order to live, so only a fool despises money. But having said that, it's got to be worked for.

I started my serious writing in 1947. My first effort was accepted in 1949, and I was paid a hundred pounds, out of which I paid ten pounds to the agent, together with £1. 11s. 6d. to prepare an agreement with Macdonald's, not forgetting the six pence for stamping it, total £11. 12s. 0d. And then, of course, there was £10 to the typist. Of course this doesn't take in the cost of the reams of paper I used in writing my story in longhand. So what was left of that hundred pounds? Only enough to pay for mending nine of the twenty-six leaks in the roof. It never was completely mended during the following five years when I still received a hundred pounds a year for each of my stories. I had thought that by then I would have earned enough also to eradicate the woodworm and dry rot with which the house was riddled. But no.

But where has all this led? It's led to eighty books being published in forty years. And what has it brought me? Money, yes. But money can't buy health . . . or kings would live for ever; nor can it buy that other priceless quality, peace of mind. I have gained some form of the latter through my work. But again, like everything else, it has to be paid for and I pay for it in exhaustion. Kind people write to me and tell me I would find utter peace instantly if I accepted the teachings in the Bible, or followed their particular path to God. Well, the answer is, I've read the book and I've tried a number of these paths and they are not for me.

Like the Scot, I must go me ain gait,
be it on mud, gravel, stone, or mossy hill.

But as everything in life has to be paid for, and fame is the dearest commodity, it's not worth the candle – believe me.

Michael Bentine and a Man of
the Church

I have never seen such an ill-matched pair. Mr Bentine with his white, fuzzy-rimmed pixie face, and the thin ascetic features of the man of the church, whose forebears I imagined could have sat on the inquisition, for his questioning was so patently subtle.

Well, after all that had been said, could Mr Bentine say he believed in a personal God?

No, Mr B quietly put in emphatically; he did not. His idea of God was love and such love as could be spread all around; and this included all animals.

Well, did Mr B believe in the seraphim and cherubim? Oh, said Mr B, there are angels about everywhere.

Oh, Mr B wasn't coming up to Church of England scratch.

Now what about hell. Did Mr B believe in hell?

Oh, yes, yes, Mr B did; but on this earth, for he had been there when he went to see Belsen. Oh, yes indeed.

I sat and looked at this happy smiling man of sorrows for had he not, besides other things, lost his son in a plane crash and his grandson and two beautiful daughters through cancer, and I marvelled at his forgiveness of sin, the sins against God that the man was so intent on getting him to admit to, at least, having an acquaintance with.

Saints come in all shapes and sizes. And there was definitely one on that programme, and he adhered to no denomination.

To a very wordy letter asking me to write a piece about 'The Meaning of Life', my reply was brief: If I knew the meaning of life I would have been the creator of it.

Language

I can laugh at some swearing, the sort that must come to the listener like 'God bless you!' But obscenities and vulgarities and four-letter words I abhor, and I'm amazed when I hear so-called cultured people using such words on the television and radio. I am particularly saddened when the user happens to be a woman, more so one, whom, for years, I had hoped to emulate.

In my raw, ignorant days on the Tyne I fondly imagined that the higher one went up the social and educational scale the more refined one's speech became.

At a cocktail party, not so long ago, a man was speaking to me about one of my books in which I had used the word 'bugger'. Yes, I do use it, but nothing stronger. But because I had used this word he must have imagined it gave him licence to talk to me as he did. For the next few minutes he punctuated his conversation with obscenities. When he used one particular four-letter word I walked away, thinking that had I heard this word in the New Buildings at East Jarrow during my early years I would have immediately rushed in to our Kate and me granda and said, 'What's blank mean?'

'Where did you hear that?'

'Mr So-and-So said it.'

Following this me granda would likely have sprung up, crying, 'The bloody, dirty-mouthed bugger! Where is he?'

'Enough! Enough! She shouldn't have been listening. Her lugs are too big.'

From the age of three I walked from the house where I was born in No. 5 Leam Lane, through the great, black, slime-dripping arches to the dock gates, there to meet me granda, and then in later years I would walk the long road from the New Buildings, East Jarrow, to the docks to go shopping. And probably on these occasions there would come pouring through the dock gates men of all trades and nationalities from captains to lascars, and not once was I stopped or did I hear one word that I thought of as obscene from any man. I did though from a woman.

Prop Annie was an eccentric creature. She travelled the roads selling props which she carried across her shoulder. The long props, by the way, were to keep the lines of washing from sagging in the middle and trailing in the dirt of the back lanes.

The young lads coming out of the docks, and some of the men, would accidentally on purpose knock a prop-end when passing her, and she would swing round, almost decapitating a number of them as she showered vile language on them. It was said she wasn't all there.

Yet the ladies and gentlemen of the television and radio are supposed to be very much all there. These are the ones who are chosen by the powers that be

74

to lead our thinking into refined channels, intellectual channels.

Give me the dockers and Annie's like; they've had no education to prostitute.

Talking to Myself

Prepare for death
By enjoying today,
For who knows,
Tomorrow someone may be saying,
Welcome! thou good and faithful servant.
Or yet again,
You may not know
If you've really gone
And left the shore;
Nothing witnessed;
Nothing seen,
Not even conscious
Of a dream.

So don't think of dying,
Give up prying,
Give up striving
To find the answer
To why you're here;
Tomorrow,
Next week,
Next year,
You'll get the call, never fear.
Don't question Fate about when or where;
They never get their dates wrong up there.

The Judge and Jury

(June 1984)

About this time I was troubled by the complexity of my character. I suppose this happens to many of us.

When in company, outwardly I appear bright, in control of myself and everyone else, apparently very mature, and with answers to quite a number of the questions relating to life. Yet the truth is, no matter how I try I cannot get my thinking to remain positive, every thought of mine has a negative side: Tom has gone out shopping; he is going to have an accident. I am about to phone someone; so I immediately hear the reception as hostile, even though no-one, practically no one, is hostile to me, at least now. I am about to ask a favour of a friend; immediately this will be refused.

On and on this kind of thinking, day in and day out, and no matter how I try I cannot get my innermost mind to run along positive lines where the consequences of a thought will be pleasant and without incident, without retaliation from someone, and without an obstacle of some sort about to confront me.

I suppose it really goes back to the beginning and the kitchen-thinking, and the outcome of my fears, bred of so many things. I was brought up with the idea that if you expect the worse to happen you will be prepared if it should materialise, whereas should it be good you will enjoy it all the more.

However, here I am, seventy-eight years old, and I know myself no more than I did in those kitchen days.

On Wednesday last, my birthday, I was toasted as a world-famous writer, yet inside myself I am as far removed from that nomenclature as I am from that little girl who, when funds allowed, would be sent for the beer. Yet, no; I am closer to her.

As I see it, fame is merely a tonic for the ego, and, as one knows, all tonics contain a percentage of poison. It all depends upon how much you lap up; overdoses can change the personality and cause you to imagine you are bigger than, in fact, you are. I may not know myself completely, but I do know I haven't outgrown my natural size.

I think it was on 26 June that I spoke the above on to tape. Today is Sunday, 12 August, and my feelings are as if it were but an hour ago that I sat here dissecting myself, for over the past days I have been gradually sinking into the trough of despond. I don't know whether those are Bunyan's exact words, but it's been decidedly a trough.

One would think that my present energy gained over the past seven weeks during which I haven't seen the sight of blood, would have taken me to the top of the world. Well, physically I am better than I've been for a long time. With transfusions, my blood count has gone up to 82 per cent where it has never been before in the whole of my life. This being so, I should mentally be up there; but apparently the brain and, definitely in my case, the body do not co-operate.

Over the weeks my body has gained energy without a corresponding response from my brain. However, the business of introspection has become keener, deeper, in fact desperate.

On Friday when at three o'clock I began to bleed again, I faced it stoically, although my reaction was that I wanted to swear; and I did damn-and-blast it for a moment or two. But then I recalled I had had seven clear weeks, and also the letters I had received from fellow sufferers of telangiectasia, some suffering frightfully from daily bleeding.

This particular bleeding of mine wasn't a 'gusher' as I term it, it was merely a normal bleeding; but I was feeling rather fragile after an hour's car ride to Newcastle in order to be dealt with by my specialist.

By now I should be used to that electric 'poker', but I am finding that with age comes apprehension. Hence this burden of introspection, not helped, of course, by the further loss of blood. It was of such a depth that I could find not one good thing to say about myself. I could have been without a friend in the world, in fact, I felt that I was, which was really ludicrous because my main aim had become the evasion of people as far as possible.

What had I done in my life? Nothing, as I saw it. I was really of no account. What were a few books?

I cried into the night. This time, Tom could not help me.

We got up; he made a cup of tea, and we went into

the conservatory and I started to cry again. Tom sat with me, begging me not to give way to tears in case the bleeding should start once more; but all I wanted to do was to cry this out of me.

Between bouts we talked, he telling me of his frustrations, I endeavouring to explain to him how I felt, when I couldn't really explain it to myself.

He summed it all up by saying it was because I was humble inside, because I knew true humility, which I definitely denied, for I don't feel humble, not as I think of humility.

'You are somebody,' he insisted; 'you're a highly intelligent individual. You have wisdom given to few, and you put it over in your work, and through this work you help thousands of people. You are somebody. Moreover, you are the only person I ever want to be with. I don't care about anyone else in the world, only you. When my mother died and Dad died, I was sorry, but that was all, it didn't really matter so long as I had you. You are somebody, not only to me but to thousands of others, and to those you would call your friends.'

At this my mind asked, who would I call friends? I have thousands of acquaintances, but who would I call friend? And do I really like them? Of all the people I know, would I really be very sorry if they died? Sorry? Yes: But very sorry? Yes; but not in the same way as if anything should happen to Tom. His loss would be so devastating that I have yet no name to put to the outcome of it.

It should happen that at that moment the Sunday papers were pushed through the letter box, and in the supplement there was a piece on Anthony

Hopkins, and the strangest thing was, it was dealing with his fight with himself, and his searching the depths for his true identity. Such had been his despair it drove him to drink and a pretty wild life. But, as he says, one morning he woke up and, there, it was all gone. He knew it had been solved, and he never again took drink, nor did he mix with the wild ones or with those in Hollywood, but, when not working, lived an ordinary life, with his second wife and daughter. He said he did not wish to see anyone, he did not want to meet anyone, he was content to be by himself.

In my case, no matter what I think about people, not being able to love them, in the way I think the word love implies, I do not want to be deprived of them altogether. I don't wish to live in isolation; yet Tom, on the other hand, for all his welcoming smile to visitors, his rush to ply them with cups of tea or coffee, and his kind words, wouldn't give a damn if, so long as I was there, he never saw anybody else in his life again. And this is an absolute fact of which I have been aware during all our married life. I've had to fight against his desire for complete isolation.

Anyway, to get back to Anthony Hopkins. He sums up his article thus: A teacher said to him, 'You may not be working out well here, but keep being who you are and you're going to get on. You are simply marching to a different drumbeat.'

Anthony Hopkins says, 'That was the first time I imagined that being different might be OK.'

And it just might be so in my case too.

I was comforted.

*　　　*　　　*

I now consider that my self-denigration must have stemmed from that child's barb, 'You ain't got no da', added to a neighbour's calling me 'a bastard', and then fuelled further by the incidents which occurred during my four and a half years in Harton Institution, South Shields, when efforts were made to sully the only thing I value, my name. Such things sink into the subconscious, to erupt later when the body and mind are together at their lowest ebbs.

Yet, I had no claim to that name. Being illegitimate I should have been known by Kate's maiden name of Fawcett; but having been brought up by my step-granda, John McMullen, I became known as Katie McMullen, and oh, how I treasured that name.

More strange still, neither of those names appear on my birth certificate.

Dog Days

It was Christmas, 1933. I was twenty-seven and I had expressed a wish for a brass helmet-shaped coal scuttle. I got my wish on Christmas morning, but was more surprised to find inside the scuttle a tiny black-and-white pup.

I knew nothing about dogs, but I soon learned. Terry, the terrier, had the natural urge of a ratter, whereby she got herself stuck up drainpipes and down rabbit holes.

The war came and evacuation, and in St Alban's Terry took a fancy to a dispatch rider and decided to accompany him . . . everywhere. There she would sit on the front of his motor-bike as if it were an armchair. When I had to move on and could not take her with me, the dispatch unit adopted her, and I later learned that her progeny literally littered the camp.

After the war came Bill, the bull terrier. I've written reams about Bill. He was really my first love and, as in most love affairs, our association was a mixture of happiness and despair. And after nine years we experienced the agony of losing him, and we told ourselves that we could never go through that again. Never!

But we must be martyrs for punishment, for some months later we acquired Simon. Oh, beautiful

Simon, a golden ridge-back labrador, who loved to roam. Again fourteen and a half years of loving devotion . . . and worry. He died in Tom's arms, as Bill had done.

Our grief was so intense that we swore, vehemently, this must never happen again.

The weeks passed, the months passed, a year passed and another six months. The house was empty . . . we were empty. Someone said, 'Get a poodle.'

What! a poodle?

Poodles weren't dogs. Have a poodle after our lovely Simon, and Bill? Never!

How can I describe our discovery of poodles. I was right from the start, they weren't dogs, they were little men, or wonderful children that never grew up.

Sandy, we called him. Everybody loved Sandy . . . except other dogs, because Sandy, like Bill and Simon, was always ready for a fight.

Why did we have dogs that always wanted to fight?

Sandy was a white miniature. He looked cuddly, but whenever Tom took him out and they approached another owner with his dog, he would whip up Sandy into his arms, only to be told, 'Oh, my dog wouldn't go for a poodle. Never! Never!' and when Tom would try to explain that this lovely-looking little fellow was driven by an urge to attack all other males, preferably ones much larger than himself, he wasn't believed.

Of all our dogs Sandy was our child. He was with us every minute of the day, he slept by our bedside at night. We tucked him in his basket, and he would wake up Tom sometimes around 3 a.m. when the call of nature troubled him. By the time he was twelve years old, the only thing I regretted was that he had never had a lady friend.

Then one night there appeared on television a pitiful sight of a tiny bedraggled poodle which a boy had rescued from a sewer. He had noticed the dog clinging to the bottom rung of the iron ladder, and he had gone down that ladder, brought up the little mite and taken it to the police station. And from there it had reached the dog shelter in Newcastle.

I was a patron of the Newcastle Dog Shelter and when I saw the poor little thing on the television I phoned the shelter to say, whatever was needed for her treatment I would see to. What happened next was they begged me to go and hold her and have a photograph taken. This was to arouse the public's conscience, because the shelter was being overrun with strays and they were having very few adoptions.

I tried to resist this appeal, but finally I found myself holding this little mite in one arm and Sandy in the other with the cameras going click, click, click. The result was I adopted Sue, and Sandy had a female friend for the first time in his life.

I have never seen such doggie love. From the very minute he saw her, Sandy adored Sue, despite her rotten teeth, vile breath, weak heart and weaker bladder and a gammy back leg. She'd had a rough time, had Sue, and was of indefinite age. One vet said four years, another said six. We ourselves imagined she must be at least ten. But what did that matter to Sandy? He never left her side. It was wonderful to see them together, she so very tiny and he in contrast looking enormous; but she always the leader.

The fact that he had her companionship for the last two years of his life pleased me more than anything else that had happened in my doggie experience.

Then that dreadful day came once more, when again Tom held our dearest friend in his arms, as he, too, passed on to join Bill and Simon. That was the most dreadful day of all, I think. And I will state here openly that we mourned the loss of our dogs as we have never mourned the loss of any relative belonging to either of us.

During the following awful weeks Sue mourned him, too. She would go round looking for him, then come and rest her head on my shoulder while making strange little noises. She was a solace to us both at that time.

When she had a heart attack the vet gave her a month at the most. She lived for almost two more years. Her heart was in a very bad state; she'd had to have most of her teeth out for they were poisoning her system; yet on she went, determined to stay with us as long as she could, because she knew we were willing her not to go, as she would be the last dog we would ever have.

How much grief can one stand? Her going tore us both apart. She, too, died in Tom's arms.

The aftermath was terrible and only dog lovers will understand this. Others will likely say, 'Ridiculous, really, for after all they are only animals.'

Again I will say, only dog lovers can understand our grief.

That was the end. No more loving companions, not at eighty-three years of age. Anyway, the compensation was that our future, be it long or short, would be free from all kinds of doggie worries: no more ringing vets, no more being woken up at three or four o'clock in the morning with a paw on your face. There would be no more sitting up with Sue after her various attacks or operations. *No more strain.* We were two old people and had to face it. But there was still work to be done.

We are a couple of lunatics . . . imbeciles, idiots. We should be locked up: in June we acquired a ten-week-old silver poodle.

What is wrong with us?

Our life is so full of work, worry and ailments we never seem to have a minute to ourselves. We don't need other human companions because we have each other. Why do we need a dog?

Su-Tu, which translated means Sue the Second, is now five months old. She is motivated by an electric current. I never imagined I'd move so quickly in my life again. She seems to have taken years off me, while at the same time bringing my demise nearer. But what better way to die than being licked to death by a highly strung, hysterical, mentally defective, possessive individual.

Sue is now eighteen months old. Her mental condition has worsened, her electric input has strengthened; she has acquired a banshee howl for coffee, which surprisingly has endeared her to Tom. Me? I have my reservations, because I have never been possessed by anyone or anything, as I am by this animal. Things have reached such a pitch that she will not allow Tom to hold my hands. Hence my reservations, for I can see a divorce pending: Su-Tu v. Thomas Henry Cookson.

I have always written Doggie letters. The following is one which Su-Tu, sensing my feelings, sent to her breeder Mrs Jeanine Stoddart, to whom she goes for clipping et cetera and to meet her mother and some of her brothers and sisters.

Sister Su-Tu,
The Hysterical Congregation of Saint Looneybin.

Dear Jeanine,
    I'm desperate. She says she's at her wits' end. Well, that surprises me, for it's a dog's tail to a wet muzzle if she's got any, or ever had any. You know what I mean? But she's blaming me for having lost them. And you know what she said the other day? I was barking up the wrong tree if I thought she was going to put up with me. Well, you know me, Jeanine, I'm as particular about trees as I am about lamp posts. That's another thing: I never get out even to see one of them for weeks on end. *He* took me with him to post the letters the other day, and believe it or not I'd forgotten what a lamp post smelt like. I've got to thank the dog gods that I don't have to cock my leg.
    A free ranger looked at me from across the road

the last time I was out, and he said, 'Poor bitch.' I said, 'You know nothing, laddie. Just look at this one I've got on the end of my lead. He's so hen-pecked, there's not a feather between him and a moulting hen. Whenever he plucks up courage to take me out, she provides him with a plastic bag and a bundle of paper hankies. Now I ask you, as if I would. And believe me, I would if I could, but I'm bunged up that end with chewing the said paper hankies. You should see her go for me – pulling them out both ends; no dignity. One of these days I'll show her, I'll tattoo her where she least expects it.

Anyway, dear, there it is. Ask the girls if they'll make room for me. Oh! the cat? Well, we'll have to see about her, won't we?

> Yours, at the end of her tail,
> Su-Tu.

PS. By the way, can you tell me what you did to my backside the last time you clipped me? It itches like mad.

PPS. The latest. She's telling people I'm mental. I'll have her up. And not only her, but all the visitors who agree with her. And this is all because I pretend I'm an Afghan hound.

Stop Press: She's losing her hair. Great do's in the house. And who's getting the blame for it? I'll give you three guesses. When you next come, will you tell her I look in need of a change?

*   *   *

Sadly, in November 1993, Su-Tu's wish came true. Owing to my worsening health and pending operations, arrangements had to be made for her to return to her breeder, Mrs Jeanine Stoddart, by whom I have been told Su-Tu has transferred her manic possessiveness on to the man of the house, and fortunately, he seems to like it.

At times I long for her and her sudden using of my stomach as a springboard in order to jump across to the window seat at the sight of a cat.

All things pass, including pain caused by doggie love.

Talking

(At the Writers' Summer School . . . Swanwick)

In the workshop of my mind, not only do I know big words, but also I can pronounce them . . . and spell them. My storehouse is unique, perfect; it is only the transport section that is at fault. Somewhere between the gem-studded vaults and my tongue is a road-house situated just above the antrum at the top of my nose. In the past, this antrum has caused me a great deal of trouble, and so, likely, this is why I chose it for the road-house where the driver halts and seems to indulge too heartily, with the result that the rest of his journey with the precious cargo of gems takes an erratic course, and when he unloads through my lips what should be words so profound as to astound even the highest intellects, what happens is that my ears, by now accustomed to astonishment, listen to platitudes so mundane as to create in me feelings of shame, for in transport invariably two syllables will have got mixed up and Mrs Malaprop appears. How I want to slay that woman! At one time she would provide me with the material for an entertainer, but such material grows stale. I was another Mrs Feather, I was told, just like Joyce Grenfell.

She, I thought, was a very clever woman indeed; but this was twenty years ago when I could afford to be a clown, for, as long as I could make people happy and laugh, what more did I want from life, at least for five minutes at a time?

But here I am now being classed as a thinker. However, there still remains the road-house somewhere near the antrum.

It is very odd about words. I could supply all the big words for anyone else; the pronunciation might leave a little to be desired, but the word was there. For instance, when Tom and I have discussions, which is almost daily, he might become stumped for a word. He can spell most words in the dictionary, but he often has difficulty in finding the right word; it is then that I supply it, and very often go on to elaborate. At these times it would seem that I have that drunken driver past the road-house, but as soon as I start congratulating myself on his sobriety, what do you think? Yes, he goes off and has a couple on the side, and comes back, dragging Mrs Malaprop with him.

Yet, put me on a platform now, before an audience of five, which I have had, or two thousand, which has been my largest, and the lorry driver makes a great detour round that road-house and everything goes swimmingly, and I lap up the responses: 'Oh, if only you had gone on talking.' And this might be after an hour or so.

The only reason for this that I can think of is: Catherine Cookson the writer, the clever bugger, is put in her place for a time, and out steps Katie McMullen, accompanied by her granda, the drunken, ignorant Irishman who can neither read nor write, and His Lordship, the 4th Earl of

Chesterfield, not forgetting Mrs Malaprop.

During that period, I gave talks all over the country, including two highlights, The Writers' Summer School at Swanwick and the Newcastle Festival.

Some years previously, Nancy Martin had asked me to give a talk at the Writers' Summer School, to which I had replied, 'What! To them? They wouldn't want to hear my kind of talk.'

From snippets I had read of the experiences of other writers in this field I had been led to believe that throat-cutting while the assailant smiled at you was not the prerogative of the scholastic world or small-town cliques, and I had had enough of that, thank you very much, to last me a lifetime.

Anyway, Nancy happened to have a daughter, and her daughter happened to have a husband, and they ran an old period house as a guest house-cum-conference-hall, and Nancy had inveigled me to go to a writers' weekend there . . . to talk. I didn't really want to go, but I went and enjoyed every minute of it. It was there, in the audience, that I met the lady who calls me her wild rose, Rosa Canina, or alternatively Lady Chesterfield, and to this day continues to address me as such. But that is by the way.

After this, Nancy got on to me again. 'Come to Swanwick,' she said, 'and give them what you gave us at Croydon; they'll love it.'

Three hundred and fifty writers loving me nattering about me granda versus Lord Chesterfield, with sandwiched between these two personalities, the struggles of Katie McMullen to be clever and to show them!

Well, accompanied by Tom, I went to Swanwick. It was the twenty-first anniversary of The Swanwick Writers' School. It started on the Saturday tea-time and finished the following Saturday morning. On the Sunday, Winsor Clark was due to speak on 'Journalism' and Richard Imison on 'The Place of Radio in the World of Drama'. Lady Georgina Coleridge would be guest of honour at the celebration dinner on the Monday (evening dress preferred). Tuesday, Elizabeth Jenkins would be speaking on 'Novel Writing' and N. J. Crisp on 'Television Drama'. Wednesday, Edward Blishen on 'Why Write for Children?' and Thursday Madelaine Duke would talk about 'Fiction in Fact'. Then to Friday: at 9.30 a.m. Dr Trevor Silverstone's address would be on 'Psychology for the Writer', and at 8 p.m. Catherine Cookson would be saying, 'She Done It'.

Talk about from the sublime to the ridiculous! 'She Done IT.' However did I think of such a title. What was worse, Mr Bill Smith was to be Chairman. Besides Nancy, he was the only one I had previously met: he had chaired the meeting of the Writers' and Journalists' Club when I gave a short talk, which, I imagine, must have left not too good an impression on him. Well, it wouldn't, would it? He was one of them, an intellectual. However, presently, I shall make no apologies for printing the letter I received from him after Swanwick.

But to go back to our arrival on the Thursday. We were getting out of the train, having travelled first-class, expenses paid, when there emerged from the next compartment a short, thick-set young man. He was grinning and talking back to someone still in the carriage, and what he said was, 'Oh, here I go to confront the madding crowd,' and immediately, I thought, 'Aye, aye! Here's one of them.' And he was.

The car journey . . . I forget who met us; I remember only that she was very pleasant and that she knew John Smith, my agent, and liked him, so I liked her. During the journey there was much name-dropping, and I tried to do my share. But who did I know? Only John Smith . . . the poet.

I remember, too, the warmth of our welcome by Mr and Mrs Boland, who were acting as host and hostess; then the surprise, shock would be more like it, of coming down to tea. Tea? Bun fight. And the noise! Long bare tables, one remembered from Sunday School treats, the end one, the high table, VIPs only. You can be a VIP this year, but next year you could find yourself in the scrum, and so it is wise not to attach any importance to it, especially at Swanwick. Quite candidly, I was amazed at the set-up, and was further amazed at the quality of the food, mostly home-grown, with home-made bread, scones and shives of home-made cake.

As I sat shouting to my neighbour in order to make myself heard I realised that this was to be an experience indeed. Later, the dinner was equally good, and after it we adjourned to the lecture hall to hear Madelaine Duke, and as I listened I grew more and more and more nervous. Is this what they expected? I couldn't compete with this type of knowledge. Later in bed, stiff, sleepless, I suddenly burst out to Tom, 'Well, I'm here, and they'll have to take what I give them, commoners and coronets. Yet wait! What about my dear Lord Chesterfield?'

Tom held me tightly and laughed, saying, 'Don't worry; you'll get them.'

I wasn't sure. In fact, I had never before in my life been so unsure . . .

The following day, from both lecturers and those on the course, I heard the same statement: 'I'm dead beat', for the real business of the day started at 9.30 a.m. and could go on, with further lectures and seminars, until 10.15 p.m. when there could be informal dancing for those still with stamina left.

I was very pleased that in between sessions people came and sought me out and told me how they liked my stories. Any writer who says he gets bored with this is a liar.

I was particularly pleased that a group of Northerners from the Newcastle Writers' Circle swarmed around me as if they were my relatives; and I felt they were. They took photos, gave me warm invitations. And this was repeated by a group from Scarborough.

All this warmth should have allayed some of my fears, but it didn't; there was still 'them' to be faced, and 'them' formed a good percentage of the three hundred and fifty.

It was now five to eight. Tom had his orders not to come near the lecture hall.

Bill Smith said, 'Well now, are we ready?' He was in a dinner suit, I in my best frock. He escorted me from the house, through the grounds to the lecture hall.

He knocked on the door, for it to be opened by Vivienne Stewart, or Alex Stewart as I like to think of her. She was a former chairman of the School and had attended for nineteen years.

She smiled encouragingly at me and patted me on the shoulder; and there I was, walking up the aisle, through the crowded hall, on the arm of Mr Smith. It was a 'last evening' ceremony, and it came to me I was being honoured.

I sat down on the platform; Mr Smith introduced me; then I was on my feet.

I had been on my feet countless times before; why should this be different? Well, it was, and as it turned out it was different in all other ways that it was possible to be different.

I looked at 'them' seated to one side, then at the would-be writers to the other; and I humped them all together and began with a backward kick to Catherine Cookson to sit down so that Katie McMullen and her trio could take over, and we were off.

Within five minutes, always within five minutes, the speaker knows whether or not he has his audience; and I knew in a strange way I had come home.

Bill Smith had said, 'Keep it to the hour'; I kept it to the hour, practically to the minute.

How good it is, how wonderful it is, to make an audience laugh, really laugh. I know how comedians must feel; but when you make them cry, what then? Now I have never had the intention to make an audience cry, but this happens, and it happened that evening at Swanwick; and later, a writer came up to me and said, 'It's the first time I've cried in public.'

Never before has a talk of mine been received as that one was. Something happened that night on that platform: I entered into all of them, and they welcomed me with open arms; and at the end of 'the ceremony', walking back through the hall, the extended hands and the applause demonstrated this.

Later, back in the house, it was all too much, the autographing of books. Swanwick afford this kindness to authors; they put their books on show. Well, I autographed mine until my fingers became stiff, and hours later I went to bed and cried, for Tom to say, 'I told you so. I told you so.'

The next morning, there was the usual rush for taxis and private cars; but even out of this chaos many spared a moment to come and shake my hand, thank me for something I didn't know I had given them. And then the final gesture: the committee, all the VIPs, formed a sending-off 'guard of honour' to our taxi. But I could not see the faces as I waved, I could only hold on tightly to Tom's hand.

And Tom; for him, it was a great eye-opener: if no-one else had thought me 'clever as owt', he had; and now he had witnessed a triumph.

At this event, I learned that it is Catherine Cookson who writes, but that only Katie McMullen can talk.

I said earlier I would make no apology for printing the letter I received from Bill Smith:

Dear Mrs Cookson,

I am sure you know from your audience's reaction just how much your talk at the Writers' Summer School was appreciated.

Although you disclaimed any intention of teaching them anything, your story was in fact a marvellous example of the grit and guts needed to become successful. When, as in your case, the talk is put over so superbly, it is indeed a joy.

Very many thanks from us all, and thanks, too, to your husband for coming along; it was a pleasure to meet him.

Yours sincerely,
Bill

I thank you, Bill, now as I thanked you then.

Why Do They Do It?

When did I first become a victim? Looking back, I think it must have been during my years as a laundry checker in Harton Institution, South Shields. I had to room with another officer. Yes, we were called officers to keep us distinct from the nurses in the adjoining hospital; we too wore uniform. Odd thought, that whenever you are put into a uniform there is a title of some kind attached to you.

The bedroom was long and narrow. Between the two single iron beds there was a small dressing-table. Opposite was a little fireplace in which you were allowed to have a fire one evening a week, and in front of which you could dry your hair. There were two single wardrobes, one at each side of the fireplace, and at the end of the room was a wash-hand stand.

The kind thoughts usually started when we were in bed, and for a long time I took them without retaliation. They would go as follows:

'Your hair's nice and thick, Mac, but it's coarse, isn't it? You'll never be able to do anything with it.'

'I liked your dance dress, Mac, but with your bust being so high it was the wrong shape really. It didn't fall properly, you know what I mean?' I didn't.

'It's odd, Mac, you having a bust like you have and big hips, yet you've got no calves in your legs.

They're just like shanks. And your knees are like winkle-pickers.'

This was supposed to be funny. But she was right, I had no calves on my legs. They were shapeless, like two sticks.

'Why did you have to buy that, Mac? It doesn't go with your colour.'

My skin was neither black, yellow, nor brown. Some really kind individual once referred to it as alabaster.

'You should never wear that type of blouse, Mac, not with your short neck.'

On and on, week after week. The climax came at the end of my second year in that room; although it didn't take place in the room itself but at the dining-table, at which ten officers were seated. And there opposite me was my room-mate who, I'd come to the conclusion much earlier, was a bitch. But having to be in close contact with her at night I had kept my tongue quiet until this day, when she suddenly stopped eating, leant across the table towards me and, a wicked grin on her face, she said, 'Ah, that's what they remind me of, you've got fish's eyes, Mac.'

Boy! Did she get a surprise. I was up before the matron the next day.

About this time I was keeping company with a young man, a pitman who was a bookie on the side, and when he had a good day he did the unusual thing for any working man in those days, and especially a pitman, he would send me a bunch of flowers and a box of chocolates. Such a response to courting had never been known, at least not in that institution.

The mess room would be all agog. When on one

such occasion, my dear room-mate, in a fit of jealous pique, suggested I must work hard for those presents, I almost threw her out of the window. But what turned out to be more effective still, I said to her, 'As long as I remain in this institution or in this room with you I shall never open my mouth to you again.'

Some months passed. One night she took ill and called out to me, I got up. Realising she was in pain with her monthly do, I went downstairs and through the bleak corridors to the night attendant, told her what I was after, then braved the blackbeetle-strewn kitchen to fill a hot-water bottle and make a hot drink.

The following morning she thanked me profusely, fully expecting this to be the breakthrough of my silence. But no: I just looked at her coolly and turned away. She again reported me to the matron. Within two weeks I was given a room to myself. Bliss indeed!

I think it was on that day I realised that if I really made up my mind to do something, I would carry it through. I had suffered for so long from her vitriolic tongue and jealousy, the while not being able to understand why she was jealous of me. It wasn't until many years later, in fact in my middle age, that I realised that at that time I had been a beautiful girl with a vivacious personality. Vanity had never been one of my sins.

I wonder if people realise the harm they do when they spit venom. For instance when you've had a breakdown you are highly sensitive to such terms as 'mental' and 'asylum' or 'looney bin'. Whilst in

Hereford I went as a voluntary patient for six weeks into what was termed 'a nerve hospital'. At the time I was neither mad nor mental; I thought I knew exactly what was wrong with me. And what didn't help was, I couldn't face up to the fact that I had 'nerves'.

I, Miss McMullen that had been, she who had weathered so many trials and tests, what had she to do with nerves? I knew, of course, that through the continued loss of blood I was very anaemic and that over the last four years I had lost three babies. But 'nerves' and even worse, oh much worse, the word 'neurasthenia' couldn't be attached to me. I did not, of course, realise then that all these terms were those commonly applied to a breakdown.

I had been back in Hastings for about a month when I met a so-called pre-war friend who greeted me with, 'Oh, you're out! I heard you were in an asylum.'

I remained dumb, and left her, feeling sick at heart with the fear overwhelming me again.

However, there are those who have made me laugh, albeit wrongly, and a little irritated, such as the business man who had to call on me. One day he asked if he could bring his wife to meet me.

'Yes; yes, of course,' I replied.

Came the day when the couple arrived and during coffee I aimed to put the wife at her ease for she seemed to have little to say.

Later, standing in the hall ready to say goodbye, the gentleman said, 'Thank you, Mrs Cookson, I so enjoy my visits.'

At this the wife turned abruptly about and

without any word of goodbye made for the front door, saying in no small voice, 'Gift of the gab!'

One laughs when one gets over the surprise and the biting of the lip and the thought, Oh, dear me! What have I done to her?

One could go on and on; but it embitters me no more; in fact, I am amused; but perhaps not when looking back to the two long years spent in that workhouse bedroom with that spitfire.

The Finger of the Gods

Some of my thoughts at night are beyond transla-
tion, too complex for me to understand, yet not deep
enough for me to think they have been touched by
the divine finger of the Gods, so bright and illumi-
nating are they at times that I am blinded with pride
of my perception as they flash like falling meteorites
across the sky of my semi-consciousness. Yet while
momentarily blinded by their surface brilliance I am
awakened to the fact that their destination is the
earth and their substance is but dull rock.

Yet, it isn't until I open my mouth in order to
impress that I again have to ask myself if I will never
learn that what the Gods' fingers write only the soul
can read, and the soul is wise and its wisdom simple
and has no need for high falutin' thought or screed.

Books are full of lives.

I Wish

I wish I were young again;
I wish my body were as young as my mind.
If I were young again,
I would be kind to it:
I would not starve it
In order to save for material things;
I would not urge it to work
Until it dropped with the pain that strain brings;
I would not, for fourteen years,
Tramp laundry floors;
I would not rob my body of rest
In order to improve my mind,
When it begged to sleep
To gather strength in the night
To meet the demands
That would begin once again
In the early light;
I would not pump into it chemists' drugs
To keep it going, the while
Knowing that there'd be a price to pay
And that some day it would fold
And say,
No further can I hold you up.

So now I ask my mind
Why it did not foretell

In those early days
What the result of overwork would be.
And its answer is derisive:
A blind man could see,
Without the misuse and abuse
You wouldn't be where you are today;
Success always leaves
An expensive bill to pay.

Age I

Where has the intensity of love gone?
The intensity to hate,
The intensity to appreciate,
All diluted, but where have they gone?
I have still within me their core:
Their seeds grew to fruition
And I used them to the full,
Up to a week ago,
Or a year or so,
Or sometime before that.
When did they fade?
When did their colour lessen?
The answer lies in my final inability to rage
Against age.

Strange Tears

I've cried in the night
Deep, silent, shuddering tears,
Tears that rend my spirit apart
And flood my heart in an agony,
While asking myself,
What is it?
What is wrong with me?
Why this pain?
What does my thinking gain from it?
Is it the knowledge I have wrenched
from life
That creates this agonising strife?
Yet, I know the answer;
So why do I probe?
Sensitivity,
Like a suppurating sore,
Was laid on me at birth.

It is many years since I wrote the above, and I know now the reason why I cried; I have suffered for years from what was termed neurasthenia. Today it bears the name of ME, myalgic encephalomyelitis, and one of its effects is bouts of crying for no apparent reason.

Royalty

That child of the Tyne; what were her dreams, when lying in the dess-bed, of entertaining kings and queens, and a princess, too?

Don't be silly. Never! Nothing so far-fetched as that. More like she prayed for a dry weekend, which had nothing to do with the weather but that funds would be so low in the house no spirit would flow or that the pawn shop wouldn't see her on Monday; but come Easter, the happy thought of perhaps a new frock, and for Christmas, a really full stocking. Shadowing all such thoughts, however, would be the ever-present prayer for a dry one, even though this would have meant no work in the docks.

So Royalty found no place in her mind, not until she was sixteen when, like every other girl, she fell in love with the Prince of Wales.

Then, as in the fairy tale, the years of hardship rolled on until one day a princess asked to call. And that wasn't all: she next asked to bring her Mam and Dad. Who was I to say no? So to coffee they came; to tea they came; and to lunch they came, when, I being who I am, no-one but myself, my banter caused mirth. I saw a worried king unbend; and afterwards his queen called me a friend.

I now ask that child of the Tyne, why she ever

doubted that fairy tales come true, although she had to wait until she was eighty-two.

With warmest regards and deepest respect to my friends, the King and Queen of Romania.

Ignorance

Saturday 29 August 1970

When I asked myself the question, had I been fortunate enough to have received a university education would I have been more wise than I am now in my sixty-fourth year? my answer was, You are going on the premiss that wisdom comes through education, whereas if you have learned nothing else you should know that wisdom comes only through trial and error, personal trials, personal errors; no-one else's experience can bring *you* wisdom.

But this quality, this perception that goes under the heading of wisdom, what is it really? What does the little bit I possess do for me? Well, all I can say is that it has helped me to accept life as it is, and, what is more, to accept death, which after all is much more important.

Another thing it has taught me is that there is nothing new in the way of thought. There have been times in the past when I have imagined, indeed I have stated, I have thought something absolutely original, such as in my teens when I coined the phrase, 'I learn daily by gaining a greater knowledge of my ignorance'. And at the time of thinking this I took credit for a clever piece of reasoning, which was understandable, because at that time I definitely was ignorant, used in the term of 'not knowing'.

The awareness of my ignorance was no surprise to me, yet I considered myself more intelligent than a number of my contemporaries. I might not pronounce correctly all the big words I had in my head, and when I did bring them out, like Mrs Malaprop, I would probably twist them about a bit. Nor was I much good at spelling; strangely I could spell a long word, whereas a short word would baffle me. I's and e's, s's and c's confused me, so when into my mind came this startling piece of logic 'I learn daily by gaining a greater knowledge of my ignorance' I imagined that I had advanced considerably in my thinking; and I went on from there. And I gave myself credit for my mental originality until many years later I happened to read 'The Apologia' in Plato's *The Last Days Of Socrates* where I came across these words 'Well, I am certainly wiser than this man. It is only too likely that neither of us has any knowledge to boast of; but he thinks he knows something that he does not know, whereas *I am quite conscious of my ignorance* [my italics]. At any rate it seems that I am wiser than he is to the small extent that I do not think that I know what I do not know.'

There was my original spark of wisdom being spoken in the year 399 BC only in a slightly different way. The only solace I received from this was the fact that I had picked up an invisible thread of thought from a man who, to my mind, was the embodiment of wisdom.

Socrates says, 'No one knows with regard to death whether it is not really the greatest blessing that can happen to a man.' He does not promise heaven and he downgrades death in that it is the least to be feared. What is to be feared, he says, is dishonesty and hypocrisy. In a way he is comparable with Christ, in that he knew if he spoke, and stuck to the truth, he would die.

After reading 'The Apologia' I knew that here were all the ingredients for a good life. I could never hope to follow them implicitly, but should I try and fail I would have no fear of his censure, whereas when I aimed to follow Christ's teachings and failed I was consumed with guilt and had to run to a priest and tell him of my sins, and ask him to ask Christ to forgive me. Of course, this wasn't Christ's fault but that of men. However, having been brought up under Catholic men, and women, I have a blockage in my mind against Christ and His doctrine.

Reading this last statement, as Socrates might, I would say that the blockage I have against Christ has been caused through the interpretation of Him, the fear engendered by man under Paul's teaching of Christianity.

To me it is the paradox that the name of Christ should be synonymous with love, for there is hardly a denomination, at least in the Western world, that doesn't punch home retribution for sin and anger of The Almighty. Even in this modern age, even when the Bible has been revised to get it over to the ordinary man and woman, fear of The Almighty still remains. Yet the paradox becomes more apparent when He is put over as the God of Love.

I could live a good life under Socrates's teaching, good without fear of the consequences of not being good, except that my conscience would be affected.

I'm sad to think that it is the Christian who has estranged me from Christianity.

So much for my grain of wisdom, which others would name heresy.

Buying Second-Hand

I don't know when I first began to wear other people's clothes. From photographs, up till I was about eight years old, I can assume I was decently put on for a child of those days, and under our special circumstances.

Not until Kate made me wear the costume coat was I conscious of how I was dressed. I don't know how old I was at the time, but I do know that I was still being sent on messages and so would have to walk from East Jarrow to the docks to go to either the outdoor beer shop, or the pawn shop, or to the butchers.

The coat hadn't belonged to Kate; it was much too big. It was made of thick dark serge, a quality material and style, but it reached to my knees. And the sleeves . . . they were spectacular. They were of the balloon kind. They were narrow at the cuff and widened tremendously to the oxter, and when I lifted my arms I must have had the appearance of a flying bat from behind and an odd bird from the front because the large buttons were in the shape of small quills. To cap all, it had a braided collar. No matter how I tried to adjust it, it would stick out like a cock's angry ruffle.

It was that coat, I realise now, that made me clothes-conscious because I was so ashamed of it, and I'm sure it was the sight of me wearing that awful coat that caused Mrs 'Swanky' Smith to stop me on the Jarrow Road one day and give me advice.

There were a number of Smiths in the New Buildings. There was 'Sweary' Smith and 'Coal' Smith and Inspector Smith and 'Singy' Smith and of course Mrs 'Swanky' Smith.

Kate did the washing for Mrs 'Swanky' Smith and it was from her, and for the second time in my life, that I heard the word 'imposition'.

The first occasion was a Christmas concert in the little Protestant school at Simonside. I can see me now on the platform, facing a little boy, almost enveloped in an outsize cap, who was holding out a basket towards me from which protruded the stuffed paper necks of two ducks. I said, 'Pray, man, how much are your ducks a pair?'

'Five shillings, ma'm; and very fine ducks they are.'

'Five shillings! I wonder you're not afraid to ask it. Pray put your fine ducks back into your basket. It's a thorough im-po-sition.'

The second time it came to my ears was when I took a basket of washing to Mrs 'Swanky' Smith with the words, 'Kate said it's three and six this week.' It had rained all week and it had taken her days to get the clothes dry. What that lady said to me was, 'Three and six! It's a thorough imposition; and tell her that.'

But here she was, on this particular day, standing in front of me in the open road and saying to me, 'Katie, I'm going to give you some advice. Get yourself away from that house as quick as you can. You'll

117

never do any good for yourself there, my dear, and you could make something of yourself. I know that. Oh my dear! make a break from them.'

I don't know what I answered her, or how old I was at the time, but I should imagine I must have been about thirteen, for she suggested that I could get into service soon.

It should happen that when my step-grandfather was in work he would come home for his dinner. Kate would stand on a cracket in order to look over the cornfield railings, which were made up of used railway sleepers, in order to see when he would appear on the Jarrow road, after coming through the saw-mill bridge. If he had been attracted to a bar there would be no sight of him, but when there was she would immediately know the minute she had to put his dinner on the table. Such was the power of the common working-man in those days that he looked upon it as his right that the meal should be ready to put into his mouth. At least, the two men in our house did, that was, the old man and my Uncle Jack.

But on this day what she saw over the cornfield railings was her daughter standing on the road talking to 'Swanky' Smith; and so I'd hardly entered the house and put down my messages before she started.

'What were you standing talking to her for, Swanky Smith?'

I recall I didn't answer her for a moment but tore off the obnoxious coat and flung it aside. Then facing her, I said, 'I wasn't talking to her, she was talking to me.'

'Yes, and what had she to say?'

'I'll tell you what she had to say,' I said. 'She told me to get away from this house as soon as I can.'

I felt very sorry the moment I'd said this because Kate's colour changed and she remained tight-lipped for a moment before she muttered, 'She meant me, didn't she? Get away from me.'

I did not answer, but I turned and looked at the coat where it covered the chair. She, too, looked at it; then she said, 'I've never hated anybody in my life but I hate that woman. I'll never forgive her for this;' then turning away, she added emphatically, '*I'll* get you a coat.'

She got me a coat; and it was new. She gave me the impression that she got it from a club, but she never took me with her to see if it would fit me. It was thick, like blanket material and slightly too big, but that didn't matter; it was the colour, no, the colours of it. The background was an off-white, the pattern was stripes and blotches of red, pink, blue. Oh! you name the colour, it was printed on that coat. I put it on once, and once was too often: I refused to wear it. It seemed that overnight I had become clothes-conscious. The costume coat was bad, but the new one was not only hideous, but also ridiculous. How she had come by this, I'll never know. What she did do next was to ask the daughter of a neighbour, who was studying tailoring, to make me a costume. Now this girl was three years older than me and, like her mother, who was the one who had called me a bastard, she had no liking for me, nor I for her, but she measured me for the costume.

There are different ways of getting one over on people you don't like; hers was in the costume she made me: it could have been made for someone in an orphanage one hundred years previously. The sleeves hung over my wrists but almost cut me under the armpits; the jacket was of such a cut it was impossible to describe it, only that it seemed to yell workhouse; as for the skirt, I could not sit down in it; and when she asked twelve shillings for making it, well, I leave you to imagine Kate's reaction.

When or how the brown costume came into my life, I don't know; that I wore it for years, I do know. It was slightly big to begin with; but I grew to it, and there came a time when the seat was so shiny, as were the elbows, that, and particularly on a Sunday morning before going to Mass, I would sponge it down and iron it to take the gloss off. And with it, I wore of all things a Henry Heath hat. It was of grey felt and had been given to Kate by a lady in Jarrow for whom she worked. It was called a Henry Heath and was in what is called a band box.

Many, many years later, when I was able to buy my hats, I would go to Mastins in Hastings for my Henry Heath hat, which would be handed to me in such a band box. Believe it or not, I still have a band box and I still have the two Henry Heath hats I bought from Mastins thirty years ago. There's a hole in the brim of one, worn away with pulling it on.

I definitely became dress conscious once I went into Harton workhouse as a laundry checker, but there were only two among the eighteen staff in our department whom I considered smartly dressed. From I don't know where I had acquired a sort of dress sense, for I could discern the well-cut and differentiate between the good material and the tawdry, and so I decided that whatever I might have in the future would certainly not be tawdry; and to this end, and bearing in mind that my wage was two pounds a month, when I saw in the window of a small but smart shop in Shields a coat priced at £7 15s., I enquired if the coat could be put on one side whilst I paid off so much a month. And this they did. They were very kind, understanding people, but it was nearly a year before I could call that coat my own, by which time I had become assistant laundress and my wage had risen by ten shillings a month. Maybe it was a long waiting time, but each month I was putting away a little money against my grandfather's funeral, and without which I knew there wouldn't be a penny, for he wasn't insured.

But came the special Saturday when I retrieved my coat. I put it on in the shop, and they packed up the one I had been wearing and, amid their admiration, I walked out and down to the Shields ferry and across on it to North Shields, where I was to spend the weekend with a friend.

I recall I was a figure of great interest on the ferry, and my friend, an elderly lady and a hairdresser, whom I had met the previous year whilst on my one and only holiday in Gilsland, was lost in admiration. She had never seen such a beautiful coat; but her reaction was nothing compared with what I received on the Sunday evening when I returned to the workhouse and the mess room. I must tell you that I was also wearing a large, a very large grey felt hat without a vestige of trimming of any kind, which was very unusual; also brown shoes that seemed to have a slight golden glow: I had painted my black ones with a special shoe paint which was supposed to be brown.

About ten of the staff were present in the mess room when I went in. Some were my friends and some were not, but all gaped open-mouthed.

I was quite frank about how I'd come to have such a beautiful coat, but did they believe me? No, not one. The next day it was round the House; the topic of conversation was Mac's coat. I understand that some said it was a scandal really, and that she shouldn't get off with it. What did they mean by that? Maybe it is unbelievable but I found out later that one of them went to the shop I had named and asked if I had bought the special coat there. Oh yes, yes; I had bought the coat there. Well, had they another one like it, enquired this certain lady.

No; they were sorry, but it was a sort of one-off, a beautiful coat, didn't she think?

What that person thought she didn't tell them, but she told her cronies in the mess room, that yes, it was true I had got that coat from that shop, but you could bet your life the money hadn't come from me.

At that time I was 'going with' a man whom I thought of then as a gentleman, and I can tell you truthfully, except paying for the pictures and bus fares, that man never spent more than a few pence on me when he had bought me a comb in a case. How I detest mean people; I must have been crazy, or something was wrong with my head, to keep company with him for almost two years following on my being friendly with the pit-lad bookie who had been so generous to me with flowers and fruit, which, as I've stated elsewhere, got my name up too.

It was this same coat I was wearing when I was interviewed by the guardians of the Hastings Workhouse in Sussex, and one councillor, a very large lady, asked, 'What do you think of our laundry? How did you find it?' and still being Katie McMullen and not yet having acquired the art of diplomacy, or the benefit and kindness thereof of white lies, I spoke the truth.

'Very dirty,' I replied briefly.

I got the job, much to the chagrin of the matron, whom I must say later became a very close friend, but on that day she pointed out that the other two applicants were much older and more experienced than I was and one held a certificate for management. Then to my amazement, yet not so much, when I come to think of it, she said, 'It was that coat that got them.'

The coat didn't help me when, a month later, I took up my position to face and organise twelve paid staff, a dozen or more inmates, and travellers from the road, all directed into the laundry for work. And being younger than any of the paid staff, the feeling of resentment, especially of the paid staff, was immediately apparent.

I was twenty-three then, and to add some age to me I had a costume made by a recognised tailor. It was of a darkish tweed, the plainest cut you could imagine, and it buttoned up to the neck. This was in 1930, mind. It certainly did add years to me.

It seemed to have an effect too, because my staff and I began to know each other and to laugh together. However, within a year, I took my own small flat, and clothes were forgotten: it was furniture now and, although I wasn't aware of it, the beginning of my collecting period: bits of china, glass or silver gradually supplementing the furniture.

When my mother joined me in 1932 I moved into two adjoining flats, the idea being to take guests. This was followed by my taking The Hurst, the gentleman's residence on the outskirts of the town. The project for it now was to be a guest house, and it could have been a very good one if it hadn't been for Kate and her bottle. When we parted in 1935 I had set her up again in the flats, on which unfortunately I was still having to pay twenty-five shillings a week because I had leased them for three years. But what was worse I had to denude my own place of enough furniture and cutlery et cetera for her to take in six people.

Life at this time was not only nerve-racking and hard but frightening. The rates were due and I hadn't the money; but I was saved by an advert in the local *Observer*: some Midland town wanted to send twenty children to Hastings to be housed for a fortnight. I applied for them, knowing that I could arrange my holidays from the laundry any time I wished. Looking back, I know I must have been in terrible straits to take on anything like twenty children who had never before seen the seaside.

Some friends, who had a bakery, were a great help, and my friend Nan also helped me when she could.

There was a clause in the agreement that the company who were sending the children wouldn't be responsible for any breakages, and I had lots of pieces of statuary in the garden. Within an hour of the children's arrival they were smashed to pieces. Oh, I could write two books about that fortnight. I was thin to begin with but I was just like two lats when they left. However, I had the rate money, and, except for Nan and her mental child, I had the house to myself, that is after I returned from work.

It was when I was taking stock of myself that I realised I looked like a rag bag. My clothes! With all the worry I seemed to have shrunk out of every garment I possessed, and they weren't many at that time. Then I happened to read in a newspaper a little advert that read to the effect that if you wanted clothes of the best quality that had been worn only once or twice you could have them at an amazingly low cost by first sending for a catalogue, enclosing a stamped addressed envelope.

At the time I was low not only in money, but also in mind and spirit. I'd had so much mental worry I was ready for jumping off somewhere. So it must have taken the form of an adventure to send for that catalogue; and oh! wasn't I lucky that I did.

It came as a rough-typed little booklet on very cheap paper. The section on dresses, each priced at five shillings, also contained a description and the measurements. Well, surely I could allow myself five shillings! I did, and waited daily for the parcel to arrive, and when it did, my! my! I was amazed. It contained a dress in a pale-green check. The material was a soft jersey, and it had a lining. What was more, it fitted me like a glove. I couldn't believe it. The bodice had a row of small buttons down to the waist; the deep cuffs had four buttons, and the skirt was pleated. All for five shillings. It was impossible to believe it. This was my first real second-hand purchase, and from then on whenever I could spare a few shillings to spend on myself, I made further purchases.

Within the next three years, right up to the war, I got some really excellent dresses and costumes from that house. It must have been a house, because the catalogue said 'no visitors', only orders by post. I have a picture of myself somewhere – I must rake it out – standing on the terrace of The Hurst in a linen costume that cost six shillings. The hat I had made, at least I had altered it from a big straw, and, all in all, it was a smart outfit. The last purchase I made from that little firm was a great box of evening dresses, ten in all, for a pound! Air raids had forced a clearing-out of stock. Some fitted me perfectly, I have the remains of one still in my wardrobe. It was made in Italy, covered in thousands of hand-sewn black sequins. I wore it once again only a few years ago, and there is a picture of me sitting at my desk in Bristol Lodge wearing this dress with the breakfront bookcase behind me. It says a lot for my figure after thirty years! After five years of the war and wear and tear, there was little left of my wardrobe.

It was after my third book was published that Tom said, 'Go and buy yourself something, *new*.'

So I went and bought myself a Jaeger suit. It was red, a really beautiful costume. I still have the coat and it looks as good as new, but style brought the skirt above my knees. Strangely, I found no joy in going into a shop and buying something which they termed new. No matter if it carried a name like

Jaeger. There was no excitement about it such as when opening a parcel from London.

Then there came the day I needed a dress to go to a function, just an afternoon dress, and Tom suggested I go to Philpott's. Now Philpott's was one of these old-fashioned shops, beautifully old-fashioned, with thick carpets on the floor and a magnificent staircase going upwards from the hall. So I go to Philpott's. Two middle-aged ladies were serving on the upper floor. The staff was like the shop, middle-aged and classy. I sat on the period couch and one of the ladies came to me and apologised, saying she would be with me in a moment, that she was seeing to this customer in the cubicle opposite. Next door to her I could see there was another customer being attended to, so I sat and waited. After taking in and bringing out of the cubicle a number of dresses, my lady attendant went downstairs and brought up a dress from a model stand that I had noticed when I was in the hall, and took it into this cubicle. But apparently the customer was very hard to please, for out she comes from the cubicle without buying anything; and she had to pass me.

My nose, although it bleeds a lot, is very sensitive to smells, and when I was in the workhouse at South Shields, young girls from the hospital would, at times, be sent down to the laundry. Most of these would have been treated for a disease, picked up likely from the sailors who came into the docks.

Now, at the time, I knew nothing about this disease or why the girls were there, I knew them only as inmates. Oh yes, I knew there was a certain smell came from them, but I wasn't enlightened as to what caused this smell for some long time later; but as that woman, the customer in this high-class shop, passed me, there it was. She was big and well dressed, yet looked somewhat blowzy.

I went into the cubicle. I tried on several dresses. None fitted; then the attendant said, 'Oh, I'll tell you what might suit you,' and out she goes and returns with the model dress I had seen hanging downstairs and which the previous customer must have tried on, and it came to me in that moment that not only that dress but all the dresses that had gone in and out of this cubicle had been tried on by her, and perhaps by countless others, too, over the past weeks, because it was the custom, I later learned, for the dresses that had been used in the showrooms, at the end of the day, to be taken downstairs to the workrooms and pressed and hung ready for the next day.

Now this set me thinking. Every frock in that good-class shop had been worn by someone else. But think of the other shops that had rows and rows of hangers with dresses which women would whip off and try on in a cubicle before returning them to their racks. Eventually they were sold as new clothes. It was a thought, wasn't it, and the thought told me very precisely that everything we bought out of any shop was already second-hand. Indeed some of them must have been third, fourth or even tenth-hand.

Thankfully, a new horizon had opened up for me. I found a shop in St Leonards that sold what was termed 'nearly new'. Madam had some very nice things, but 'the house' was too close to the grammar school and would have embarrassed Tom, so I went

128

farther afield, to Brighton in fact. I had come across this source by accident. It was held in one large room above a high-class business premises and presented models from France, Italy and London. They weren't cheap; no indeed, but that didn't matter. They were of beautiful cuts and material and I felt great excitement in visiting that room once every three months.

There was no excitement attached to the thought of dining out in posh restaurants or of going abroad, but I got real excitement about that regular trip to Brighton. I bought things that I didn't need but was happy to pass on to different friends who knew nothing about the source, of course. They only knew that I had money now and would, of course, buy the best.

I can honestly say my visits to that room were the only thrill I had in my life at that time. Then they almost stopped. I did a programme on the television, and I wore one of my smart pieces; and so, imagine my dismay when next I visited the room and the proprietor said, 'Ah! Ah! I saw you. We saw you; the whole family saw you; and you looked lovely. It was a smart piece, wasn't it? All this time you've never said who you were. Well! Well!'

I was to learn that I wasn't the only supposedly famous customer who bought second-hand.

I was in Pinewood Studios, sitting on the grass next to a well-known actress and waiting for one of the hangars to be emptied. One of my Mary Ann books had been filmed, and I was there to do a romance day with John Gregson. This had been commissioned by a magazine, and as the actress and I sat talking I remarked on the lovely dress she was wearing, at which she laughed and said, 'Poor thing! It knows the lot of us. I think I must be its sixth wearer here. But isn't it pretty! And the odd thing about it, it seems to fit different sizes of us.' Then she told me that not one of the actresses she knew could afford to buy model gowns, and that there were certain shops in London where one could pass on, as it were, their clothes.

So why should I worry? I didn't; and so I kept up my exciting visits to the room until we left the South for the North in 1976. Just imagine the outcry had it been known I was fitted out by a second-hand shop.

However, I was fortunate in finding a good-class, not second-hand, shop in the centre of Newcastle. It was called Enid's. It was small and select. They fitted me out with some beautiful clothes which, in a way, weren't much dearer than those I had obtained from the room in Brighton. Unfortunately, Enid's went out of business; but later I found a very select establishment set up in a lodge on the outskirts of Corbridge. They too fitted me out with some beautiful things. My last purchase from them was for the day I had to open the Catherine Cookson Building in the Medical School at Newcastle University. It was a two-piece: a black wool dress that was so simple it looked to be a straight bag until one put it on. It was a lovely cut. Then there was the coat. It was a winter coat, very unusual, double-breasted and flowing with tight wool cuffs and collar. Very unusual. The only time I get the chance to wear that coat now is when I am being taken to hospital. I always wear it over my dressing gown. It may be covered with ambulance blankets but that doesn't matter, I love the feel of it and to know that I am wearing it once again.

It was shortly after I made this last purchase that this shop, too, went out of business. Like the little corner shops, I am sure it is greatly missed; but almost from the day following the opening of the Catherine Cookson Building I was forced to my bed, and for the most part there I have remained since, except for crawling out of it to take on three special occasions.

One was a birthday do. It might have been for my seventy-eighth or somewhere about there. I think it was to do with my book *The Black Velvet Gown*. I recall trying to get a long black velvet gown but without success, so I had to plump for a silk dress with winged sleeves. It was very smart; and after a fine lunch, there I was on the platform accompanied by the dignitaries of the day and facing the long room packed with guests. At this point I should put in that I hate such do's, the main reason being that I'm always expected to speak and to make my audience laugh. It's a difficult business, you know, making people laugh, especially those whom you've seen year after year and who must have heard the same thing over and over again, so you try to rake up something different; and that's what I did this time. It was certainly different.

After the usual opening giving the reasons why I was standing there and they were sitting there, I startled the ladies by asking if they knew that perhaps every one of them was sitting there in second-hand clothes. Oh yes; there would be hardly a new rag among them. All right, yesterday, when they bought the rag they might have been thinking it had actually been made for them. Well, yes; had they not bought it at a very select shop? Yes; they had, but before they'd had the chance to look at it, a few others had likely been in and tried it on.

My narration didn't go exactly as I'm stating it now, but that was the gist of it; and I went on to tell them of my experiences, from Kate's costume right up to the last special outfit I had bought, knowing that the previous evening it had likely been down in the workroom being sponged and pressed, and, what is more, it was likely one of a half dozen of the same model now spread over the country. I asked if they'd ever bumped into another woman wearing the same frock, no, not a frock, the same model.

Well, the result of that talk was very surprising: later, there were a few confessions, and we had a good laugh about our exploits.

But my shopping days are over for second-hand or otherwise. All that's left for me now is to lie here staring at my wardrobe that holds pieces I would hate to part with yet know that I shall never be able to wear again. However, they recall to my mind the days covering a number of years, during which the only excitement I allowed myself against the monotony of work were my visits to Brighton and that special room.

Reading

The following was written at the request of Lady Antonia Fraser for the book *The Pleasure of Reading*.

When did I first start to read? I don't know. I can only recall when I was first aware of reading: I was sitting in the corner of the kitchen and was startled by Kate's (my mother's) voice yelling at me, 'I'll put that book in the fire! Get it out of your hand.'

Would it have been my 'guilty' book?

I attended Simonside Protestant School from when I was four-and-a-half until I was nearly eight years old, when I was taken away to attend a Catholic school, 'in order to learn the faith', as my granda put it.

While at my first school I had borrowed a book called *The Chatter Box Annual* from the caretaker's daughter, and became so enamoured of it that I couldn't give it back. I re-read it until it was thread-bare. The result was that for years afterwards I couldn't look at that girl whenever we passed on the road, for I knew I had stolen her book.

I must have been athirst for something to read when I committed my first real theft. Funds were very low in the house at the time, for I hadn't a penny for my weekly comic *The Rainbow*. I had been sent to the newsagents for a paper and in the process of picking it up from the counter had managed to cover *The Rainbow* with it. However, after its perusal I suffered torment, knowing that I should surely go to hell for stealing; and I'd already had a taste of that region through my nightmares: my sins had caused a missionary priest to send me from the confessional staggering worse than my granda did when he'd had a skinful, for on that occasion the admonition had been, 'It's a wonder you're not in hell's flames burning, child.'

In 1919, following a hip injury, I left school. I was thirteen years old. It was at this time, too, that the first real book I'd had of my own was given me by the woman upstairs. It was *Grimms' Fairy Tales*.

When I was fourteen I read *A Girl of the Limber Lost* by Gene Stratton Porter; and following on this came Charles Garvice, Ethel M. Dell, Arnold Bennett and Hugh Walpole. Yet I remembered snippets of Shakespeare, first from school, recited from the blackboard, and further snippets of his sonnets from a collection of 'Literary Books' which a stockily built Scottish lodger kept on top of the chest of drawers in the bedroom.

I have fond memories of my little intellectual docker, and often wonder what he would have become if he'd only had the chance to do something other than unloading boats. I also recall being forbidden to look at these books, and when Kate caught me reading Shakespeare's *Venus and Adonis*, declaring it to be mucky stuff, I couldn't see it – it was only about kissing! And the people weren't real.

My first experience of real reading took place at

twenty when working in the South Shields work-house as a laundry checker. I had started there when I was eighteen, following on two years of a one-man business of penpainting, the only profit accruing from this having been lead poisoning. So I felt I was very fortunate in getting a job in the workhouse. Being a strong Catholic at the time I imagined that this was what God had intended me to be – a checker at the workhouse laundry: two pounds a month, all uniform found, four square meals a day, and every other night off. What more could anyone want?

I had been there three months when I began to question God. I felt He had slipped up with regard to my future. My thoughts now seemed very sinful, touching on pride, thinking I was cut out for some-thing better. But what?

Culture!

At the time, I did not think of it as education, I only knew that ladies were what is called 'cultured', and my first aim was to be a lady and 'talk proper'. But you had to have accomplishments, such as music and languages. I could already play the piano – a bit. I had been having lessons for a year when I was thir-teen, but the day the post brought my examination result to say I'd passed my first exam with distinc-tion the men came and took away the piano as our Kate was more than somewhat behind with the payments. Anyway, at this stage I could not have practised the piano, which was in the officers' – the staff were officially called 'officers' – sitting-room, for the rest of the staff wouldn't have stood for it. So I did the next best thing: I went out and bought a second-hand fiddle, for a pound. It was in a case, together with a bow and a lump of resin; and I took lessons at a shilling a time and endeavoured for six or nine months to conquer it before having to face up to the fact that there must be something wrong with it . . . I couldn't play it!

The next piece of culture was French; and in the study of this I was very unlucky in the choice of a teacher. Another 'shilling a time' went bang, for she couldn't get my accent right.

Before intellectual enlightenment hit me, I recall, I studied phonetics and Indian clubs! I must really have become proficient with the latter, for I developed in places that remain with me to this day.

At this time I was still a strong Catholic, and therefore my reading was constricted to some extent. A book by Elinor Glyn entitled *Three Weeks*, which was banned by the Church, was going the rounds of the staff, and the popular quote was 'He did but kiss her little feet', which always evoked uproarious laughter, from which I deduced it was a 'mucky book'.

I was never slow in voicing my opinions, and 'my table' knew my thoughts on mucky jokes and mucky books; and so some of them must have consulted the devil and therefore were prompted to leave in my room a book called *The Career of Catherine Bush* written by this same bad woman, and in a moment of weakness I fell, and read it.

I've often said that I think Elinor Glyn was put on this earth for the sole purpose of enlightening an abysmally ignorant north-country girl, for it was in this romantic story the duchess tells her secretary that if she wishes to further her education and become a real lady she must then read Lord Chesterfield's *Letters To His Son*.

To say that my life changed at this point is absolutely true. I could not wait to get to the library – it was my first ever visit there, I must confess – and I took out volume one of the earl's *Letters*; and from then on a new world opened up for me. I was given my first taste of mythology, history and geography, and in going through further volumes I was introduced to names of authors such as Voltaire, Plato, Pope, Swift, on and on. I wish I could say that I read all the books that were mentioned in the *Letters*. Many of those I got from the library were beyond me: I was never one for skipping my reading, but I found more than a few of the books verbose and boring. Now, of course, I realise it was because at that period of my life and ignorance they were beyond my comprehension; and yet I must also remember I had so little time to persevere in studying them, my years during the 1920s being daily filled with hard work.

It wasn't until I married in 1940 and was evacuated to St Alban's with my husband's school that, for the first time in my life, I had time, eighteen months in fact, in which to read, really read, and I was fortunate that our little flat was right opposite the library, which from then on actually became my university, with my dear Lord Chesterfield as my tutor.

But again I must recall that it was during my twenties that I became acquainted with a number of French writers through a French guest – I had a guest house on the side while still managing a laundry. She introduced me to *The Pasquier Chronicles* by

Georges Duhamel, and then to the short stories of Guy de Maupassant and to Voltaire's *Candide* – in translation, of course. I tried recently to read again *The Pasquier Chronicles*, but found the flatness of the writing actually did bore me.

Yet it was not until after the war, while struggling to overcome my breakdown, through writing, that the fruits of Lord Chesterfield and my past reading became a valuable asset. I had learned from Chesterfield's *Letters* that every word he wrote expressed itself. There was no hyperbole, he was a writer of plain English, so I aimed to pattern myself on this particular worthwhile asset, and I may say he was the only writer from whom I have gleaned any practical help. An odd review or so has likened me to Dickens or Hardy. However, my circumstances had been such that I never encountered either Dickens or Hardy during that first search for culture; now that I have I must confess to not enjoying their work. As for the Brontës, I did enjoy *Wuthering Heights* and *Jane Eyre*; of Jane Austen, I enjoyed *Mansfield Park*, more so than *Pride and Prejudice*. I have enjoyed, too, Steinbeck and Salinger and books such as *The Robe* by Lloyd C. Douglas, and *Raintree County* by Ross Lockridge. If I have any regrets, it is not that I did not go to university, but that I had no guidance during my late and formative teens.

When I began to write about subjects of which I was, at least partly, cognisant, I had to study nineteenth-century social history, and in this I was greatly helped by books written by Arthur Bryant and G. M. Trevelyan, and, oh yes, *A Singular Iniquity* by Glen Petrie in which he deals with the life and work of Mrs Josephine Butler. I also gained much from my reading of *Faithful* by S. G. P. Ward when dealing with the First World War. Then when I 'took my characters to Texas' Fehrenbach's *Lone Star* and *The Comanches*, two amazing books, helped me to understand the country and its people much more than did the plodding through books of American history.

In my search for God during these latter years I have lost count of the books I have read. Many only succeeded in heightening my doubts, but *The Christian Agnostic* by Leslie Weatherhead, a very tolerant man, helped me, as did the reasoning of Paul Renan and the philosophy of Thomas Aquinas. I say tongue-in-cheek that I went through the philosophers from Plato's *Apologia* to Brian Magee's *Great Philosophers*, for this latter might be looked upon as a reader's digest in this field. Incidentally, I have to say that Mr Magee's expositions on television brought my delving among the philosophers into focus more than my previous reading had done.

And then there is dear Rabbi Lionel Blue who plays God's idiot, centre stage, and whom I consider to be the best advocate going for his Master.

I had a spasm of reading Indian and Chinese writers, and others, but I wasn't in search of a guru, they were too much like priests. And after all, I'm one of those northern big-heads who want to think things out for themselves, an 'I've done it all on me own, lad' type – woman know thyself. At last I can say this, and the knowledge of my ignorance is still heavy upon me.

I haven't yet touched on poetry. This is a matter

of individual choice, more so than is one's taste for prose.

I've been scribbling rhymes since I can first remember. I would not dare to term it poetry. Even today I am inclined to 'view' and to read much modern poetry simply as 'prose on short lines'. The first poem I remember, and which frightened me, was Longfellow's 'The Children's Hour', especially the verses:

> I have you fast in my fortress,
> And will not let you depart,
> But put you down into the dungeon
> In the round-tower of my heart.
>
> And there will I keep you for ever,
> Yes, for ever and a day,
> Till the walls shall crumble to ruin,
> And moulder in dust away!

This haunted me for years, for I did not connect it with love.

Nowadays I dig into all kinds of poetry and lately was very touched by a collection of poems written by soldiers in action during the Second World War and called *Poems From Italy*.

The longer I go on writing this the more books are coming to mind, books that I enjoyed but had forgotten. It is inexcusable that I should not have mentioned them, but what do you expect from a doddery old girl of eighty-four whose mind drifts back to the time of *The Rainbow,* and Katie McMullen (myself) sitting in the corner of the kitchen reading while unconsciously taking in the atmosphere – such as our Kate reading Philip Gibb's report from the Western Front to me granda who could neither read nor write, but who wanted news of the place where his only son was fighting. He never drank his beer while he listened, but when it was finished he would blow the froth off the top of his mug on to the red hot bars of the fire where it sizzled. He would then hand me the mug to have a sip before emptying it himself.

> I have you fast in my fortress,
> And will not let you depart,
> But put you down into the dungeon
> In the round-tower of my heart.

My favourite books

Lord Chesterfield's *Letters To His Son*; the short stories of Somerset Maugham; *She*, Rider Haggard; *The Forsyte Saga*, John Galsworthy; the books of Leslie Weatherhead; *The Little World of Don Camillo*, Giovanni Guareschi; the *Rogue Herries Chronicles* of Hugh Walpole; *The Catcher in the Rye*, J. D. Salinger; *The Grapes of Wrath*, John Steinbeck; books by Rabbi Lionel Blue.

Coping

From my unknown father I inherited something called HHT, Hereditary Haemorrhagic Telangiectasia – a very rare vascular trouble. Its first tangent was anaemia, but we didn't categorise tiredness under that name eighty years ago.

Should I baulk at being sent 'a message' or doing another task by saying, 'I'm tired, our Kate,' – our Kate was my mother – the answer I was invariably given was 'Work it off. You'll cope.'

Then one day in 1985, as I was assiduously correcting my work, I found I was reading with my head well to the side and the print wasn't so clear as usual. I put a hand over my left eye. Oh, I could see all right. I put a hand over my right eye. I remember getting to my feet startled. There was nothing there except a sort of light at the side.

Within two hours I was in hospital and going through tests.

'I'm afraid', said the specialist, 'you've had it as far as this eye is concerned,' or words to that effect. It transpired that one of the HHT had burst in the back of the eye and there was nothing could be done about it.

Anyway, I recall I came out of that hospital very dismayed. Apart from a little peripheral light in my left eye, I had only one eye. The effect was strange, to say the least. I felt for a time that I was only half the person I had been.

I was finding that the peripheral light from the dead eye was interfering with the good one. The wearing of an eye-shade was suggested, but I couldn't take to it. I could still see; that was the main thing.

I was writing more than ever now, publishing two books a year and stock-piling others. My brain was a machine that had to be constantly oiled with words.

I may say here I was only able to work at this pace because of the invaluable assistance given me by my husband in all ways. He nursed me, he cooked, he advised, and if possible he wouldn't allow anyone but himself to do anything for me. It has always been like that. So he went on unselfishly giving me his life, and I went on working it off and coping.

During this period constant bleeding was lowering my resistance, so when one day the peripheral light from the left eye seemed to take over and mix the print on the page, it was time to pay yet another visit to my optician.

He is a kind man, my general optician, and did not inform me what was happening but took the course of giving me 'stronger' glasses, four pairs in a short time. Then one terrifying day the print on the page was obscured by a light fog. It was as if someone close by had been smoking.

Again the specialist was at my bedside. He was kind but frank. 'You're eighty-four, Mrs Cookson,' he said, 'and I'm afraid you have what age brings, macular degeneration.'

Grandfather as baby

At Harton
Institution,
Tyne Dock,
1924-29

With other
officers of the
house staff,
1924-29

New Buildings – East Jarrow Victory Tea, 1918

Standing in what was the kitchen space of 10 William Black Street after demolition. Behind is back of Philipson Street

Showing front of Philipson Street down to Cissie Afleck's shop before demolition. The backs of the terraces can be seen running at right angles

My favourite photo of Tom –
punting at Oxford.
These were his happy days:
he was yet to meet me. Poor soul!

A memory of Hastings – 60 years ago

How I looked during
the period 1937-1940,
when I rarely smiled:
a bitter period.

Evacuees at
'The Hurst', 1940

Taking Mother to the
dentist, just before
she died in 1955. I look
upon it as the day she
slipped the leash and left me
dumbfounded –
Oh! Kate, Kate.

My first painting: Tom the Gladiator.

Rigged out in my second-hands: ready for London and my publisher

Loreto, Hastings, 1973. In bed again, but still working

Loreto, Hastings, 1973. Result of planting 20,000 bulbs over the years

This Is Your Life

Being presented with a Million-copy Award for
The Mallen Streak by my publisher, Paul Scherer, 1982

Myself, aged 77 at Bristol Lodge, Langley, with Tom
and our wonderful Sandy

Then his next words nearly caused me to vomit in front of him. 'You won't go actually blind, you'll still be able to make out shapes,' he said.

Oh God, I'm going to be blind. The word blind screamed in my head. I, Catherine Cookson the writer, whose life depended upon her writing – at least her mental stability depended upon her using her brain and the only way she could do that was to write – was going blind.

OH GOD.

The specialist's voice came to me as if from a long tunnel saying, 'You can get all kinds of magnifying glasses that will help you to read, at least for a time.'

AT LEAST FOR A TIME.

YOU WON'T GO ACTUALLY BLIND, YOU'LL BE ABLE TO MAKE OUT SHAPES.

'How soon will it come, I mean . . .?'

He knew what I meant and he said, 'Oh, in some cases it's a gradual process, in others . . . well, you can't tell. But don't worry, you'll find ways of coping . . .'

I WON'T! I WON'T! NOT WITH THIS. My lips did not voice the screaming in my head. Cope, he said. Cope. I'd been coping all my life. Work it off, Kate had said, you'll cope. I had so far coped with various body illnesses, with losing four babies, with going almost mad in a breakdown, and here I had been in bed for the best part of four years owing to continual bouts of bleeding, together with neurasthenia, and I had coped. But no more, no more. This was the finish . . .

Some days later, around two o'clock in the morning, I was sitting up in bed. Tom was still holding one of my hands. He could say no words of comfort for we had discussed yet again the visit of the young man who had called with four different kinds of magnifying apparatus, from the usual hand ones to one that looked like a television, but the impeding slowness of the appearing words irritated me beyond measure.

I looked to the future. There wasn't any. By this time I couldn't read a line. I could write but I couldn't see what I had written, nor, worse still, could I remember exactly what I had written.

I had always had a wonderful memory, but this now was seemingly being affected by the loss of my sight.

WORK IT OFF. YOU'LL COPE.

Not any more, Kate. Not any more.

Another saying of hers came to my mind, 'God will provide, lass. God will provide.'

GOD.

What had God done for me? Hard work and grind all my life, coupled with most of the illnesses my body could take and the mental torments of shame and rejection. He hadn't left anything out, had He? GOD WILL PROVIDE.

He had provided for me all right.

I had never been given to self-pity because I knew there were people physically a thousand times worse than myself, and mentally too. Whatever had been thrust on me had been countered by my being given the power to cope.

COPE, BE DAMNED . . . THAT WORD! Well, this was one time that I wasn't going to cope. I was a writer who couldn't write, I was a painter who couldn't paint – during the previous few years, under Tom's urging, I had taken up painting again just to give me a break from my daily and incessant routine. What was there for me to do now? Sit here in this bed waiting for Tom to read the mail to me? To read the headlines? To do the crossword?

No, I wouldn't have this; and it didn't help me when a friend who should have known better said, 'I've no idea how you must feel; I only know if it was me I wouldn't be able to stand it, I'd finish it.'

Not having listened to radio programmes for such a long time, one night I switched on haphazardly to hear some men talking, and to my astonishment it dawned on me that they were blind. Each described his reactions to approaching blindness. The effect on me, pun-wise, was very enlightening. No longer did I feel absolutely isolated. These were men talking, and telling, each of his own particular agony.

I switched off and asked Tom to look up the title of the programme. It was *In Touch*. And a comforting phrase came into my mind regarding these men: the camaraderie of the blind.

From this time, it seemed that a light did appear at the end of the tunnel. I had become increasingly distressed about the sorting out of my food on the plate, no matter how Tom might have arranged it, and the feel of a messy table napkin could almost bring me to tears. Also I was forever picking up small non-existent black objects from the sheet or the bed cover.

Thankfully, through listening to *In Touch* I was assured that this was just one of the phobias

147

of approaching blindness.

Whereas, for months, my mind had been dwelling on an easy way out, I now returned to my 'inner voice' that had always guided me. Call it soul or subconscious or spirit, whatever, it had, in times of great need, given me answers to my despairing questions, answers which, at the time, did not seem to apply to my present need but which turned out to be right in the end. And this time, to my plea, it said, 'Go on putting your stories down on tape,' and I cried back at it, 'What's the good? I can't correct them,' to which came the answer, 'Tom can read them to you and you can dictate the alterations to him, and just as you used to delete and scribble alterations between the lines, he can do the same.'

So it came to pass that I ordered my days: beginning with the mail, Tom would read a letter to me, and I would dictate back to him my reply. This generally took the whole morning, when there were no interruptions. After lunch, we would carry on in the same way with the typescript of a story.

During any break I would return to the tape and continue to dictate my tale.

The last thing we do at night is the *Telegraph* crossword.

Of course, nothing runs this smoothly: often HHT interferes; at times, too, we both feel exhausted and cannot go on, Tom at eighty and I at eighty-six.

The main thing is, I am indeed working it off and coping again, and I say with assurance that I can now look ahead to the time I have left in knowing that I may continue to provide some measure of happiness or entertainment for my readers, the while I myself am being stimulated by what I hear each week listening to In Touch.

Finally, I would say again:

BELIEVE THIS

You're winning. You simply cannot fail. The only obstacle is doubt; there's not a hill you cannot scale once fear is put to rout. Don't think defeat, don't talk defeat, the word will rob you of your strength. 'I will succeed.' This phrase repeat throughout the journey's length.

The minute that 'I can't' is said, you slam a door right in your face. Why not exclaim, 'I will' instead? Half won then is the race. You close the door to your success by entertaining one small fear. *Think happiness*, talk happiness, watch joy then coming near.

The word 'impossible' is black. 'I can' is like a flame of gold. No whining heart. Eyes! look not back; be strong, O Will, and bold. *You're winning though the journey's slow*; you're gaining steadily each day. Oh! Courage, what a warmth and glow you shed along the way.

This poem is by Minnie Aumonier, author of *Gardens in Sun and Shade*.

Macular Degeneration

The wagtails on the lawn,
The white horses breasting the lake
In formation making for the beach
Where mallards lie preening,
And rooks crow against the wind
That bend the branches that cleft their nests,
And I store the scene
Against the time when the mist will take over.

The Plan

(1 June 1990)

The gods drew up a plan
For a special woman and a special man,
And ordered it to be governed by the stars.

The stars now mapped out the dates
For the birth of the woman and that of the
    man.
The woman they sent first to earth
In a storm of shame,
For she carried no man's name;
But they fashioned her a character
With a will to fight
The stigma of the blight.

The man they nourished a little longer,
And, whereas his stature was not tall,
He was good to look upon,
And his brain was keen.

But still the gods directed their fate,
And willed they should not meet
Until the need in both was great,
The woman through thirty years of strife and
    pain,

The man alone inside . . . in spite of his brain.

To their own kind on this plane
They both appeared oddities in their way,
As different in temperament as night from day.
Yet when, by seeming chance,
They came face to face
Recognition was as swift
As a lightning race.
It was as the gods had willed
When they drew up the plan
For that special woman
And that special man.

For fifty years they have let them stay
Supporting each other day by day.
And the pair, in their way being wise,
They do not try
The will of the gods to bend,
And ask to know the end.

Humility

He never talks about his own achievements,
He never brags about what he can do:
He would paint the house inside and out,
He would rip out dry rot, and paperhang,
Strip lead pipe and wipe a joint,
Lay tiles on the roof and replace a gutter,
And all without a mutter,
Sustained only by cups of tea.
And in the evening . . . never taking a fee . . .
Tutor one not so smart in maths in order to
    see
He'd have a chance in life;

Then in bed, reading Ancient History
Or more often Latin Odes . . .
I didn't like this pattern,
For what did I know about Latin?

This went on for years.
Now at seventy-six, has he altered? Not a bit.
Only changed the pattern,
For, between the cooking, shopping, and
    seeing to me,
He returns to his books, to Domesday now,
From which with wrinkled brow
He translates the Latin into English script,

And for a change, still
Dips into history of far-gone times;
And never a word about what he does,
Or can do,
While I,
Passing my time in weak rhyme,
Am acclaimed.
No humility here,
I just glow,
Which goes to show
Humility doesn't pay.
But would I have him any other way?
No.
Yet there is one thing left to me:
I can blow his trumpet vol-un-tar-ily.

All right, it is weak verse, but not to show my
appreciation would be worse. Some men
wither inside while waiting for such words,
and women grow old and bitter because 'I
love you' has never been said to them. The act
in bed is the mainstay of creation, and it may
satisfy the senses but it does not feed the
heart.

Love needs the instrument of a voice.

Tom 1975

We have been married for thirty-five years. We were married on 1 June 1940. Dunkirk was being evacuated at the time. In a way the war was just beginning, our own private war, fought against a loving friend and my mother, had ended. This particular war had gone on for three years. Sitting in the train on our way to his people we couldn't believe that we were together as man and wife.

Anyway, our first year together was one that all romantic girls dream of; but I was no romantic girl, I was thirty-three years old and during that period I lost my first baby. Even so, it was the most wonderful year, and not a little due to the fact that for the first time in my life I had someone to look after *me*, work for *me*, a man who at the end of every month handed me his pay cheque. You would have had to be brought up amidst the Northern working class to know that you were experiencing a miracle in this one particular case. And from that first pay cheque until his last when he had to retire through severe migraine six years ago he always handed me his cheque, which if I remember rightly was £32 a month immediately after his demobilisation in 1946. We had a joint account then, we have a joint account now. There has never been any yours and mine, it has always been ours.

I look back to what I did with those cheques. I always pride myself that I could make a penny go as far as a sixpence.

The fact that Tom handed me his earnings each month is even more remarkable when I realise what he went through because of lack of money when he was up at Oxford. He went up on an exhibition and altogether he was allowed £150 a year. His stepfather was out of work, and his only support from his family was moral. When in 1936, towards the end of the slump, he put in for the post at Hastings Grammar School he was one of four hundred applicants, so when he finally did have some money you would have imagined he would have hung on to it like grim death. But no, he handed it over to me. If I didn't love him for anything else I'd have loved him for that. I can forgive most things in most people except meanness, because if they're mean in pocket they're usually mean in spirit.

Never once in our thirty-five years together have we wished to be separated from each other, even for a day. I followed him round during the war, putting up with landladies and conditions both good and bad. Twice I lost a baby in digs. I would suffer anything rather than be separated from him, and suffer I did. But there were some laughable times.

In one temporary digs Tom said he was bringing another RAF fellow in the following evening to coach him in preparation for a test. The fellow knew less maths than I did, and that's saying something. The following evening the visitor had hardly taken a seat at the table when the door burst open and the landlady cried, 'Now not two of them! I'm not having any hanky-panky in here.'

When she was confronted not only by Mrs Thomas Henry Cookson but also by Miss McMullen, who had managed women for fifteen years and was very much on her dignity, she apologised, went out, to return five minutes later with a can to say she was going down to the local, did we want any?

Then there was another temporary abode, our bed-sitting room so situated that I had to go through the kitchen-cum-living room to get to the lavatory, and seldom did I make that journey but my landlady would say, 'By! I've been through it again today; it's the neck of me bladder, you know.'

On wash-day she would hang out on the line in the enclosed backyard, vests and pants and knickers so old, so riddled with holes that I wouldn't have used them for dusters, and she confessed to me they had only one change of clothing. I think this was in the hope that I would hand some of mine out, for I knew she had been through my cases.

On the day Tom was posted to Hereford and I was taken by ambulance to the hospital in Grantham where I was to lose my second baby, the family car was waiting at the kerb to take them on a holiday. It was an old car, granted, but so was the underwear.

A fortnight later, I was in Hereford, where I was to stay for three years, and not happily, fighting illness all the time.

There is an old-fashioned saying, 'You are making a rod for your own back', and at times I wonder if our love for each other had taken on the shape of a rod, for now, when we're in the last quarter of life, there is a fear in both of us of what will happen to the survivor.

I have been aware of the uncanny knowledge for a long time of the year in which I will die. I say to myself perhaps it's just wishful thinking or imagination, yet the date persists. But no matter when we go, soon or late, one before the other, this I do know, we shall never be separated.

(The date of my death has long passed. How we torture ourselves.)

The Gladiator

I was in the corner seat of a compartment waiting with Tom for the London train standing in Charing Cross to get us back to Hastings: it was a window seat. Tom was sitting opposite. The long corridor carriage was made up of four-seat divisions with a partition between each. There was no-one sitting next to Tom, but my companion was what I called a London gent: immaculate blue suit; his bowler, umbrella and briefcase on the rack. I couldn't see his face, it was immersed in *The Times*.

On the other side of the gangway sat four ladies who had evidently been up to London for the day. They were of the 'Ladies Circle' type, hat, gloves, suit, generally tweeds. This, by the way, was in the Fifties.

Although I was aiming to read, I was aware that outside on the platform, within a side glance, two men were standing. I could hear their laughter through the small open window above the large pane.

Except for polite twitters from the four ladies the carriage was quiet.

Then breaking into this near silence, and actually lifting me from my seat, was the sight and sound of my husband springing up and straining his red angry face towards the narrow aperture of the upper window and yelling, 'That is my wife you're discussing, sir!'

If he had come out with a mouthful of filthy abuse I could not have been more surprised, astounded, and even frightened.

Here we were returning from a fortnight under so-called canvas. For some reason or other that I cannot recall, we had earlier left the scout troop to return to Hastings after summer camp in the care of the GSM. I think I might have had to see my publisher; I can't recollect. When I entered the train all I knew was I was weary and longing, longing for my bed, for I had been lying for a fortnight in a four-foot high-ridged tent in the New Forest, sequestered from the camp itself because females weren't allowed too near the scouts' tents; in fact, I was under censure for having the nerve to follow my husband. But during these past two weeks it had rained most of the time and I had bled every day, which occasioned my spending most of my time propped up against a box and a rucksack. My only diversion was painting and erratic visits from Tom and young scouts, who must have been longing for a sight of their mothers. Anyway, I felt depleted and ill. I knew I looked colourless, and I felt colourless. As for vivacity, that had gone with the wind and the weather.

Moreover, let it be understood, I, like the year, was now in my fifties. Yet, there was my husband yelling through a train window at two strange men, 'That is my wife you're discussing, sir!'

I found myself half across the table, clutching his arm and hissing, 'What is it! Have you gone mad?' and he hissed back, 'Didn't you hear them?'

160

'No, I didn't hear anything. Hear what?'

What could they say about me? There they were standing on the platform still laughing.

The compartment was no longer silent: the four ladies were looking across at us, making murmuring sounds; heads were being lifted over partitions; one man walked up the gangway, looked at the little fellow in scout uniform, then walked back again. And all this while the London gent kept his head well behind *The Times*.

I sank back into the corner and stared at that fellow sitting opposite. Had he gone mad?

That is my wife you're discussing, sir.

What had they been referring to about me? Could it have been my hat? I had a weakness for hats; I went in for those with very large brims and their opposites with veils. Yet today the hat was ordinary, a straw, nothing to cause any comment.

As the train was about to move I turned my angry gaze away from my husband to the window, to see one of the two men boarding the train. They were both laughing.

I was feeling slightly sick . . . more than slightly. The London gent turned over a page of *The Times* and I saw that he had a thin ascetic face. I could imagine what he was thinking about the couple he had been landed with.

Silence followed, for how long I can't recall; then there was a stir. It came first from the four ladies opposite, in slight gasps. And then the reason for it nearly stopped my breath, for, swaying into the compartment was the gentleman from the platform. He had two empty glasses in one hand and a bottle in the other, and after placing them on the table, he looked across at me with a great wide grin on his face and flopped down beside Tom, whom he ignored, as he did the man behind *The Times*, only now *The Times* had been lowered.

It was when the inebriated idiot went to lean across the table towards me that I sprang and the London gent gave vent to a loud, 'No! No!'

Tom had half risen, his fist doubled, and as I caught his arm and cried, 'Tom! Please! Please! Don't!' there was a concerted movement from the whole carriage.

My body half over the table, I thrust the gladiator back into his corner. Then I turned and glared at my would-be admirer, and at this he made a sound in his throat, staggered to his feet, picked up the bottle and glasses, had some trouble in opening the door, then disappeared for ever from my ken.

He was a tall fellow, all of six foot, very well dressed, but I knew that if one of Tom's fists had contacted that man it would have levelled him, for my gladiator had had quite a lot of experience in boxing.

I knew I was in a state. My body was shivering visibly, and my eyes were shut tight when a very kindly voice said, 'Don't distress yourself.'

I opened my eyes and looked at the London gent. His expression was kind and his voice was soft. I couldn't speak. I watched him fold up his paper neatly and lay it on the table and, like that, he continued to sit quietly.

I daren't look at that fellow across from me for there was rising in me a feeling amounting to rage.

He had embarrassed me; he had made an exhibition of himself; and for what? The fellow was drunk. What had he said to make him so mad? Anyway, no matter what it had been, it was being said about a woman in her fifties.

Men didn't make passes at women in their fifties.

Well, he had, hadn't he?

But he was drunk. Likely he wouldn't look the side I was on if he had been sober.

Was it because Tom had a thing about drink?

Was it because he knew I had suffered from it since I was a child, had a breakdown through it, that my life had been marred by it? But of late he had gone too far. He had even expressed his opinion strongly that priests or parsons shouldn't drink.

'What about the Holy wine?' I had asked him.

To this he had said, 'A substitute of some kind should be used.'

At Tunbridge Wells, the London gent gathered his things together; then, looking down at me, he said quite nicely, 'Goodbye.' He said nothing to Tom.

But at Bexhill when the four ladies rose to depart, one after the other they came across and with wide beams they nodded at Tom and said, 'You did quite right, sir. You did quite right.'

'Yes,' said another; 'you acted as you should,' and she, looking at me, said, 'You can be proud of your husband.'

Proud of my husband? I could have killed him at that minute. I have never been able to stand scenes. Having been bred on them, I now can't tolerate them. And this scene had been out of all proportion to anything I had so far experienced during our married life. He knew that I met dozens of men in the business of publishing. Hardly a month would pass that I did not go up to town to have lunch with one or other of them, because those were the days when lunches went on the expense account. But he had never shown the slightest bit of jealousy. Sometimes, I felt he was taking me for granted, although I knew he loved me dearly. He felt sure there was only him in my life, and there he was right. So why on earth had he gone berserk about that drunken idiot? and in a trainful of people, for after the fracas there had been lots of toing and froing up and down the aisle to the toilets.

We got off at Hastings, we got in the bus, we got home and I never opened my mouth. But when I did I simply said, 'I'll never forgive you for embarrassing me like you've done today,' to which he answered, 'Didn't you hear what he said?'

'No, I didn't.'

'Oh, then I'd better not tell you.'

And he never did tell me. But reasoning it out afterwards, whatever the man had said it was definitely something he had meant to carry out when he brought his bottle and glasses in. Yet what he expected to do in a crowded train God only knows.

But seriously, this reaction of Tom's affected me deeply. He had been so furious. Recalling the expression on his face, he looked as if he wanted to kill the man; and his actions could have been such as would have got him into court.

When, the following day, two friends came to visit us and realised there was something unusual in the atmosphere, and I explained to them what had happened, they actually doubled up with laughter, and the female said, 'Instead of getting into a paddy you should think yourself damned lucky at your age being able to create the atmosphere of a duel. Oh, I wish I'd been there. I wish our Bill would do something like that.'

Strange, but I've never been able to see the funny side of that incident. It had been unexpected and showed a facet of Tom's character that I never imagined was there. But I was to see it surface again and again. This quiet man who, apparently, gives the impression to everybody of being so kind, gentle, patient and courteous: opens doors for scrubbers and duchesses alike; stands up immediately for the same type on one or other entering the room; carries ladies' luggage; and drives a car as a gentleman should . . . a man like this could never lose his temper. No, he doesn't just lose his temper, he releases a fury, and causes a brawl in a railway carriage!

The Day of the Drain

Two episodes have caused me to laugh. One I always refer to as the day of the drain.

We lived on an unadopted road, and so it was necessary for us to keep a drain running the 300-feet frontage of our land. It needed to be 2 feet wide and 1½ feet deep to take the surface water. It had to be kept clear twice a year if we did not want the overflow to rush down our very steep and winding drive straight into our kitchen. It was what would have been termed a navvy's job – the silt had to be shovelled out, put in a barrow and carted away.

It should happen on this particular day that a lorry was collecting the debris from a house opposite us which was being demolished; and what does the driver do but back his lorry across our newly cleared drain, breaking down the sides.

There was no-one more surprised than that driver when this little fellow tried to open the door of his cab as he yelled at the big man inside, 'Come down out of that! Come down out of that, I said, and see what you've done.'

The man could have laughed, but as he looked down into the little fellow's face, he must have seen something there that kept him in his seat. And the lorry spurted forward and through the gates, and I had a job to stop the gladiator from following him: I kept shouting at him, 'It's done! It's done! We'll tackle it tomorrow. Come on!' I had to drag him down the drive.

Half an hour later there was a knock on the kitchen door; and there stood a six-foot huge lump of brawn with a spade in his hand.

He looked down on the gladiator and said, 'I've fixed it, mate. It wasn't intentional like; the road's so bloody narrow it's difficult to turn.' And then, standing back, he added with a grin on his face, 'By, if I'd got out of that cab; you looked fit to scalp me. Bugger me! but I felt safer where I was.'

I couldn't believe my ears when, in answer, I heard Tom saying, 'Would you like a cup of tea?'

'I wouldn't mind, mate, I wouldn't mind.'

I left them to it in the kitchen; I had to get away quickly because I knew my laughter would become hysterical and would likely end up in my having another bleeding. Laughing or crying, away it comes.

So much for the gladiator: Would you like a cup of tea?

Hold Your Horses

There was another occasion when the Gladiator showed his zeal, and it happened to be linked with the same drain. It was a very hot Sunday afternoon and we had just finished mowing that 300 feet of footpath that bordered the drain and on which we were encouraging grass to grow. I had run the mower over half of it; then Tom had taken over. The machine was a 12-inch cutter that would go when it was pushed, and it needed some pushing. It must have been one of the first ever made; we had bought it second-hand. Everything in those days we bought second-hand, even the watering can, at a sale. It was heavy laden with cement with which someone had endeavoured to plug the leaks, and seemed to weigh half a ton without the water.

Anyway, to get back to Brigid, as I called the lawnmower. Tom had just pushed her through the gate at the top of our steep drive – the only time she ever ran smoothly was downhill – and we were halfway to the house when we were both brought to a stop by the muted thudding of horses' hooves. Brigid was immediately thrown to one side and we both rushed back to the gate. But the gate itself was like a ten-foot farm one and by the time Tom got it open the riders were well away. But that did not deter him from standing in the road and yelling after them, 'Keep off my path!'

'It's no good,' I said, 'they can't hear you. You're wasting your breath.'

'They'll come back,' he growled.

I didn't think they would, but by the look on his face I thought I'd better stay and referee the coming combat.

They did come back, and on our pathway.

'What do you think you're up to? We have just finished mowing that path. The road is for horses, not the footpaths.'

The older girl moved off the path into the road, saying very sweetly, 'Oh, I am sorry.'

This brought down a few of the Gladiator's ruffled feathers, until her younger and pretty partner grinned down on the little fellow, as I'm sure she saw him, and in the cockiest of tones said, 'It's an unadopted road. We can ride where we like, and we're going to.'

As he sprang for the horse's head she was a second before him by digging her heels into its rump, and, insult added to injury, she kept it on the path.

I thought he would take off.

The Gladiator has always held women in deep respect; but from that day he excluded those on horseback. From then on he only had to hear the sound of horses' hooves on the road above and he would go up that drive with the speed of a frustrated stallion to get at them.

He never caught the cocky young lady; but what was noticeable afterwards was that the riding schools which made use of the road kept to it.

However, this did not stop his immediate reaction to the sound of horses' hooves . . . Never misjudge the capabilities of a small man; besides possessing a knowledge of boxing, this one had at one time been a quarter-miler!

Help

I've always maintained that, apart from reading, I've had help from no-one, that I am where I am today through my own efforts, through no-one else's, either monetary mentally or physically; but recently I've begun to think back, and I realise I've had help from a number of sources.

There was, for instance, Thomas Henry Cookson, a schoolmaster. I learned a lot from him, because he brought his blackboard home with him, and I went to a sort of evening class, that didn't pass without heated exchanges, I may say, between master and pupil: I soon discovered I wasn't the only one with an enlarged ego.

Then there it was again, when he was a river sailor, knowing nothing about boats, insisting on being captain of the 28-footer the while going up the wrong side of the river, with me hanging on to Bill, our bull terrier, who would whine like a banshee whenever he sensed danger. Neither of us could swim.

And there was Thomas Henry Cookson the gardener, an expert with rhododendrons and azaleas and who showed me how to use a spade, also to cut down a tree, debranch and saw it up; he himself had an antipathy towards saws.

There was also Thomas Henry Cookson the cook,

who after retiring and taking over the kitchen would not take advice of my experience of thirty years at the culinary art. But this I didn't mind, for what he taught me then was never to look a gift horse, or two, in the mouth.

I'm not sure about the time when I was in need of a day and night nurse, but I recall I learned a lot about patience and uncomplaining tenderness at this time.

But what I prize most about Thomas Henry Cookson and me is the friendship that has grown stronger during the last few years and which stems from the mainspring of love which began when I married the teacher, the gardener, the sailor, the cook, the odd-job man, the secretary and the chauffeur, the day and the night nurse, and the friend, fifty light-years ago. And for this voluntary service and inestimable help I can only say, from the depths of my heart, Thank you, Tom, for you and your ego.

Anniversary

Darling, what can I say
On this your special day
That I haven't said before?
Darling, what can I give you
On this your special day
That you don't already have?
I want to eulogise,
Be witty,
Make you laugh
That silent mirth of yours;
But all I can say
On this special day
Is simply, I love you.

I'm glad I'm alive
To feel my aches and pains;
I'm glad I'm alive
With another day to struggle through;
Simply, my dear, because I have you.

Love

I read love in your gaze;
Would that it could my pain erase.
I feel love in your touch;
Would that it could ward off fear which troubles
    me much.
I feel love in your smile;
Would that it make living worthwhile.
I feel love in the selfless thought you daily expend;
Would that this go on until the end.
I exist only because of you;
We are one in ailments, too;
No separate beings, for I gaze on you with love,
    touch and smile,
And the response from you is as mine.

These are my thoughts at night when, exhausted,
    in bed
I lie;
But the gods be willing, we shall see the dawn,
And hopefully the day will be bright;
And we shall work, talk, argue, and laugh a mite,
Until again it will be night
And the weight of the day once more will be
    expressed
In mournful rhyme.

Why do I do it?

The Candle

His love is like a candle in a dark night;
It is a star in a sunless universe:
The single flame glows for me alone;
It radiates warmth that comforts my soul.
When, tired of the struggle, I give in to
    despair
It is there,
Beckoning me to its flame;
But should there come a time
When I find the distance too far,
I know the wick would bend,
And the candle, too,
To see me to the end.

PART TWO

The In-Between

The Odd Happening

We moved from The Hurst to Loreto on the 5 November 1954, Guy Fawkes night. It was pouring from the heavens. We were weary and tired in all ways; then such a nice thing happened. A knock came on the door, and there stood a doctor, father of one of Tom's pupils, with a large hamper. In it was a hot four-course dinner. A wonderful gesture.

I had forgotten to say that, at the time, my mother was with us. The previous year, the prognosis of each of two doctors had been that she had but a fortnight to live, and so I had brought her to Hastings from the North-east. But she had a year in The Hurst and two in Loreto. However, I recall that night and her joy in unpacking that hamper, because food was the second love of her life . . .

All the rooms needed redecorating. Whilst living in The Hurst, through necessity, we had learned to do all the work ourselves, so we were continuing here. Tom had progressed from painting to plumbing and wiping joints, patching roofs and breaking, single-handed, through 12-inch walls to insert glass doors.

But what about the odd happening?

It was on the night before Christmas Eve, Tom was perched precariously on a plank laid between two step-ladders. He was papering the bedroom ceiling. I had handed up to him one end of a long strip of pasted paper – all wrong, we now know! – when, hearing a strange noise, I said, 'Listen! That's Bill.'

Bill was our bull terrier. He had, up to a minute beforehand, been sitting in the room watching proceedings. The sound he was making now wasn't a bark but a deep, deep growl, and it was coming from the landing. When it was repeated, then followed by the most weird sound like a long painful, drawn-out whimper, I dropped my end of the pasted paper, oblivious to the fact that it was now enveloping Tom and that he was emitting cries that certainly weren't whimpers; and when I reached the landing there I saw a strange sight. Bill was standing on the half-landing looking down the main staircase. A bull terrier's coat is very short but it seemed that every hair on his body was erect, both his ears were upright, whereas one had always had a permanent droop. His whole body looked rigid.

I was yelling now, 'Tom! Tom! Come and see this.'

My husband was of a very sceptical nature, he believed only what he saw or what could be proved through mathematics. Now he came out of the room pulling pieces of wet paper from his hair, but what he was going to say to me was checked when he saw the dog.

We both walked slowly down the short flight of stairs and stood behind Bill on the landing. 'Go on down, boy,' Tom said quietly.

Now in The Hurst I had played a game with Bill and we had continued it since we came into Loreto:

180

Bill would sit on the top stair and I would put the sole of my foot gently on his hind quarters and push him, and then he would go down to the next step, and so on. When I was in a hurry it became very awkward to get downstairs. But now, when I put my foot against his bottom, he refused to budge. Tom again said, 'Go on, boy. Go on down.' But still he made no response. The dog was staring fixedly at something at the foot of the stairs and whatever he was feeling was being transmitted to us. And it was intensified when suddenly, without any pushing, but his body still rigid, he began to walk very slowly down the stairs, and when he reached the foot he stood still, with his head well back as if he were looking up at something or someone.

Another thing, we have never been able to get him to sit to a command, we had always to put a hand on his rump. And so what we were witnessing now was enough to make the hairs stand up on our necks, it was just as if a hand were being placed on his rump for he slowly sat down, his head still well back; and then, his whole body relaxing, he lay flat with his front paws stretched out; and so he remained for some time still seeming to be looking at someone.

When at last he stood up, he turned and looked at us, wagged his little stump of a tail, and walked off.

It was from this incident that I felt the presence in the house . . .

During the Christmas holidays we worked from morning till night, scraping, painting and papering, and it was about eleven o'clock on New Year's Eve and freezing with the cold that I left Tom upstairs still at it, and came down to the sitting room to get warm. My mother was tucked up in bed next door; she hadn't been too well for some days. I pulled the chair close up to the fire and, with my knees almost on the bars, I sat there thinking, New Year's Eve! and here we are still at it. Do we ever do anything else but work? We must be mad.

I was feeling very tired and low, and it was as I straightened up and went to sit back in the chair that I became still. Then turning my head slowly I looked behind me and I heard myself saying aloud, 'It's all right, Miss Harrington. Don't worry, we'll look after your house. I'll make it beautiful for you.'

I hadn't been thinking of her but I know that at that moment she was there; her presence was as strong as if I were seeing her.

I felt no eeriness as I said to her, 'Go in peace.'

It wasn't fancy on my part that she lingered until Tom and I stood at the open doorway listening to the bells ringing in the New Year.

I may say here that Miss Harrington had had the house built to her design in 1938, and had died in 1954. She had been ill for a long time and had left the house and its contents to a nurse who had been with her only a short time, and the nurse sold it to us. I think Miss Harrington had loved the house.

This was the first of the odd happenings.

The Second Odd Happening

Bill's experience and mine were the first of the odd happenings. The second took a quite different form.

It was in the early Sixties. My mother was dead and the room in which she died I was using as a study. I was well established as a writer. It was more than seventeen years since I'd had the breakdown and my mind was under control except on those occasions when, due to overwork, I suffered bouts of what I called exhaustion. Then, the buried fears would erupt.

But on this day, it was towards the end of November, a very dark, very wet day, I left the study to go upstairs; but when I reached the half landing I was brought to a halt by the feeling of being enveloped in a scent. Not a smell, a scent. It was as if it were emanating from some beautiful flowers. I looked at the sill of the tall landing window to my side. On it was a vase, but it was empty. The garden was bare; the trees leafless; the creepers on the wall pruned back to the last inch.

One of the tangents from my breakdown had been that I could not bear the smell of any kind of scent. It had the power to make me feel sick and often gave me a headache, and that's one thing that I've been thankful for, I have never suffered from headaches.

I recall looking down at my dress. I took the

handkerchief from my sleeve, only straightaway to ask myself what I was doing. I never wore scent, did I?

Slowly I walked up the next short flight and into the bedroom; and the scent was still with me. I told myself not to be afraid, that this was something that could be explained.

The scent faded away, and as I stood looking out through the rain-smeared window I decided to say nothing of this to Tom.

However, some months later, while on a visit to the North-east, I spoke about this experience to a doctor friend, and he laughed and said, 'Oh, I used to imagine things like that when I was a lad, it's to do with the sex glands.'

I didn't believe him. I was nearing sixty and I'd had a normal sex life, and thankfully still had.

Besides being allergic to scent, I was also allergic to the smell of cigars. Cigar smoke could make me feel faint, and almost pass out, whereas the smell from a pipe I found pleasant. So, about three years later when, sitting at my desk in the study, there should surround me a smell very like that from a cigar, I was amazed to find it pleasant.

On this occasion I told Tom, and he believed I had experienced these scents. Since the business of Bill and whatever he saw at the foot of the stairs, Tom had lost a great deal of his scepticism.

It was about 1973 that we had an extension built on to Loreto. It was 30-feet long and formed a large study-sitting room.

This particular day I was at my desk answering fan mail, and there it was again, a perfectly beautiful aroma. I called out to Tom who was sitting on the couch at the far end of the room, 'Can you smell anything odd?' And he answered, 'Smell? No.'

'Walk down the room,' I said, 'and tell me when you do smell something.'

He stopped within a few feet of my desk and exclaimed, 'Good gracious! Yes, I do smell something, a very pleasant smell, a kind of perfume.'

We looked at each other; then I said quietly, 'Go back to the couch and see if it spreads with you.'

He started, but almost immediately said, 'No: it's gone.'

'But you smelt it?' I said.

'Oh yes, definitely,' he said, 'but just by your desk.'

Well, the comforting thought at that moment was that it wasn't the outcome of my imagination, someone else had experienced the smell. And I consoled myself further that this phenomenon wasn't an everyday happening, in fact there had been years in between my experiencing it.

We left Hastings for the North in 1976. My health was deteriorating fast; my blood trouble had worsened.

During the following years I suffered two severe heart attacks and three minor ones; and so, altogether, I had become well acquainted with hospitals in Hexham and Newcastle.

Then once again I found myself in what I had come to think of as my room at the RVI in Newcastle. This time I'd had laser treatment for internal bleeding and was not feeling very bright.

Tom used to come early in the morning and stay

with me until I insisted he leave before dark for that 30-mile ride back into the hills.

On this particular Saturday I'd had other visitors; but now I was lying quiet when one of the nurses came in, only to stop at the foot of the bed and say, 'What a lovely smell! Have you got some scent on?'

'No,' I said, 'I don't use scent, not as a rule.'

Whenever I have been tempted to put a drop on my wrists, I have immediately had to wash it off.

'It must be the soap over there,' I said.

She went to the wash-basin, picked up the soap, shook her head and said, 'No, there's no smell from that.' Then she looked towards the window-sill. 'You haven't any flowers either,' she said.

'No, I haven't any flowers, for at close quarters they make me sneeze, and you know what happens when I sneeze.'

'Funny,' she said, 'but there really is a nice smell about.'

This talk of scents, however, did not worry me at that moment, because I couldn't smell anything; and there were other things on my mind, such as 'popping off' and what would my dearest Tom do then? A short while later, the door opened and two nurses, standing there and laughing, said, 'What have you spilt in there? You can smell it out in the corridor.'

'I haven't spilt anything,' I said. 'It must be the soap.'

Still laughing, they came in and picked up the soap; then shook their heads, saying, ''Tisn't this; but it's a lovely smell.'

'It's the blood you're likely smelling,' I said.

'Go on with you!' they said.

Oh dear, dear! Not that again. And I lay asking myself why, on this occasion, I couldn't smell anything.

The night staff came on and my two favourites came in.

'Oh, there you are!' was their greeting. 'What have you been up to now? Oh, and what a lovely smell! Have you had flowers in?'

'It's the soap,' I said.

Some more sniffing.

'No; it isn't the soap. You could smell it in the corridor.'

'Well, it's from the corridor, bedpans likely.'

'Oh! Mrs Cookson. Surprised at you!'

On and on went the chit-chat.

Then around eleven the night sister came in. She was one I hadn't met before.

'Good evening, Mrs Cookson. How are you?'

'Oh, not too bad.'

I waited for it; but her remark came in a different form.

'This is a nice room.' She looked around her. 'Such an air of peace in it.' A long pause and then, 'So glad you're feeling better,' and out she went.

The following day was Sunday, my day for fighting God; but I was too weak to bother. Tom came in just after nine. I told him what had transpired. He just shook his head.

'I would like to get to the bottom of it,' I said. 'It's no use asking doctors. I'll get the sex answer back likely. But why couldn't I smell anything last night?'

'Yes,' he said, 'that's a point, why couldn't you?'

It should happen that Father Tom Power of Haydon Bridge drops in at home now and again. As I have told all the others of the cloth I have told him he is flogging a dead horse, but he still maintains I'm a Christian of Christians.

At visiting time who should come in but himself.

After we had chatted a bit I thought to myself, I wonder if he has ever heard of this phenomenon, so I said to him, 'Father, over the years, I have periodically had a strange experience. Not very often, but now and again I smell the most delicious scents. But from yesterday this scent has apparently surrounded me, and everybody except me has been able to smell it.'

Before I had got this far his eyes had widened, and now the most tender smile came on his face and he said, 'I knew it. I knew it. I've been telling you for ages.'

I actually cried at him in no small voice, 'Don't you start sticking me up with the saints again or I won't believe a word you're saying.'

'Don't believe me,' he said, 'read the life of Saint Thérèse of Liseux. The very same thing happened to her.'

'Look, Father; half those women were up the pole,' I said. 'Obsessed with religious mania or frustrated sexually. Anyway, I'm an agnostic, as you know only too well. Oh! Father,' I said, 'I'm not up to arguing with you; I'm a poor sick woman.' He smiled as I said this. 'But as far as I can gather,' I persisted, 'it isn't my mind that is sick it's only my body, so it's no good trying to drum into me there's a pair of wings waiting for me if I'd only conform.'

He laughed outright now and, looking at Tom, he said, 'You're with me, Tom, aren't you?' And being a hypocrite, Tom said, 'Yes, Father.'

Well, there it is, the odd experience of the scents. As for the explanation of the Saint Thérèse business, that, to my mind, would be utter presumption and the last result I would expect from my way of thinking over the years. Not only of thinking, but of fighting for what I believe. So, what is the answer? Mental aberration or hysteria? I don't know.

Yet, I'm sure not all those nurses would have been suffering from hysteria.

The Experience – The Third Odd Happening

A miracle? Oh no; yet I don't know what name to put to it; I know only on that particular Sunday I was in hell, the kind of hell in which I had lived for some years following on a breakdown in 1945, when I was thirty-nine years old.

At that time I was riddled with fear reaped from seeds sown in times past, covering childhood, youth and middle-age. I lived hourly in depression and anxiety, added to which was a deep feeling of aggression. It was as though I wanted to retaliate for what I had gone through, and yet I was constantly fighting this urge for fear I would do something desperate. Added to this, my body was weakened with the daily loss of blood from the inherited HHT – Hereditary Haemorrhagic Telangiectasia. This had caused anaemia and neurosis, which I would not recognise, for I classed this, at that time, as being linked with insanity . . . I wasn't odd. I wasn't going mad.

I look back on that time as being in Hades, the underworld in which no light glimmered. It was the black night of life and my rope ladder of will-power had swung far out of reach. It was ten years before I could clutch the bottom rung. But during that period how I worked at my writing, being a schoolmaster's wife with its attendant duties, and looked after and cleaned The Hurst, only God knows. My heart had definitely forgotten how to sing, if ever it had, and my smile was a façade, my body powered in the locomotion of pain from my attendant complaints.

Yet throughout this time of intense suffering I begged no help from the Son of God; rather, I continued to fight Him off. He had been a torment to me for years, my mind ever questioning His omnipotence and omnipresence. I had even stopped pleading with His mother, begging her intercession, for from a child it had been drummed into me that the only hope of getting in touch with Him was through her.

I've always stated I suffered ten years from the breakdown. What I should have said was, it was ten years before I began noticeably to feel some relief. Gradually such periods lengthened, but even up till the Sunday of the experience short bouts would recur.

Ill-health too, began to have its effect on my physical body and eventually forced me to spend most of my time in bed.

In 1989 I contracted the dreaded 'flu', which took me into deep depression, and I was swept back to the breakdown. No small bout this, but this was different: my mind in part was quite clear. I knew what I would have to do. I could not fight this alone now, as I had done before, I would have to have help.

For days I lay inert; but my mind was planning my future: when David, my doctor, should come tomorrow, Monday, I would tell him that I must go into a hospital . . . a nerve hospital, not a mental

191

hospital. No, no! The very thought frightened me further. Definitely I was back in 1945.

I hesitated to tell Tom what I was planning. He knew I was in the depths, but my going away would mean separation, and such is our feeling for each other that wherever I was, he would want to be with me; in fact, he would insist on being with me.

It was three o'clock on the Sunday afternoon. I was lying like someone lifeless after an attack of neurasthenia, which at times partly paralyses me. No amount of will-power could make me move or speak when in one. But here I was lying inert when a voice, as if from a distance, said, 'Get out of that bed!'

I took no notice; the mind plays tricks on one. When it came again, saying, 'Get up!' I answered it: 'How can I?' And again it said, 'Get out of that bed and walk.'

It was as much as I could do to walk to the bathroom which was en suite, and then I often had to be helped. But the voice came once more, saying, 'Get out of that bed. You're not in an attack now, you can move.'

'I am so tired; I have no energy,' I said. 'You know I have no energy.'

Again it came, 'Get out of that bed. Put one leg over the side, make an attempt.'

'What then?' I asked.

'Go into the sitting room and look at the television.'

Oh dear God! Look at the television. I couldn't bear the television these days; everything was so trite, so meaningless.

But I found myself sitting on the edge of the bed.

Langley, Northumberland, 1983. Taking in strength from my beloved trees

A rare day: aged 79. I had got up and dressed to receive Brian Enright, the University Librarian, and three young people I was starting off in the binding department. I recall it was a happy day

Painting

Watercolour of Venice

Drawing of Lichfield Choir

Addressing 150 guests at my 80th Birthday

With Russell Harty at my 80th birthday celebrations

Morning coffee with my beloved friends

Morning of D.B.E. day with the beautiful basket of flowers sent to me
by H.R.H. The Prince of Wales. In life there are highlights.
This superseded them all.

Writing, 1986

OBE, with Tom, 1986

Receiving Doctorate, 1991

With Tom and
D.B.E. medal

The Thinking Years

'Walk,' said the voice.

I stumbled about the bedroom.

Tom came in. He's never surprised at anything I do, but he was aghast to see me shambling down the long room.

He led me into the sitting room, where silently I made for the television. He switched it on, then knelt by the side of my chair, holding my hand.

I recognised the programme as a repeat of *The Railway Children*. There was nothing to disturb me in that, I'd seen it so often. I paid little attention to it for my mind continued giving me directions on what I must do on the morrow and how I must break it to Tom, because I could fight this no longer on my own. I was at the end of my tether. It had been a long tether, but there was nothing more to hold on to. My will had gone, except the part that was arranging what was to be done.

I must have sat a long time before I realised that *Songs of Praise* had started. That night it was from Buckfast Abbey. Someone told the story of the brothers and how they had built it. There was the stonework and the long nave. Tom was kneeling by my side, still holding my hand, and he said, 'Would you like a cup of coffee?'

I nodded, and he got up and left the room.

Now the cameras were moving up the aisle towards a huge stained-glass window, until the screen showed only the face of Christ. It wasn't a nice-looking face. It's difficult to make a nice-looking face out of pieces of glass, but there He was.

I don't think I had moved since I had first sat down. But as the eyes looked into mine I suddenly thrust out an arm and placed my hand flat on his face the while I cried from the depth of my tortured being, 'HELP ME! PLEASE HELP ME!'

NOW, I know that I am a writer of fiction, that I have an imagination, but no imagination of mine could ever conjure up, or make me feel, what happened in the next moment. No, not in a moment, in a split second, in a time that would take lightning to pass before you, or strike you down, so quick it was. But I cannot explain it.

Don't forget I had no faith of any kind that would demand cures or miracles; all that I had reasoned out of myself. But there I was, as free from fear and filled with such a feeling of peace that, as Paul said, passeth all understanding. Such was it, I could put the word exquisite to it. I was uplifted, freed from all torment; I was, in a way, made whole.

At this point, realising that Tom was standing at the door of the room, I turned my bright shining face towards him and he called, 'I know! I know! I felt it in the kitchen.'

As he hurried towards me, I cried, 'I'll never question Him more. Doctrine, yes; everything else, yes; but never Him. I believe, and never again will say, help thou my unbelief.'

I sat savouring the peace. I had never experienced anything like it before in my whole life. The agony of my mind was as if it had never been. Yet, only too well I knew it had been, and had consumed me.

Tom looked as happy as I felt. And the feeling that was on me told me I could and would cope with anything that might hit me in the future.

Within a few hours this was to be tested.

However, before this I had sat in a state of deep tranquillity as I told Tom what I had intended to do on the morrow.

It should happen at six o'clock on the Monday morning I started to bleed like a pig. It was from both nostrils, and immediately I knew it was a 'stinker'. This meant an emergency trip into Newcastle. Tom phoned Hugo, Mr Marshall, my specialist. But when Tom went to get the car out he could hardly make out the garage across the yard, the fog was so thick. This added to his panic.

He always gets into a panic when I bleed heavily as I was doing then. He dashes round, first ringing my specialist and getting the poor man out of bed again, which Hugo has done so willingly over many years, then dashing round the house locking up here and there, and seeing to the dog. Lastly, he drags on over my nightie what he calls my 'bloody coat' – it has been drenched so many times – and puts a woolly shawl over my head. Then sets the alarm.

But this morning he came back to me in a real panic. 'I can't see the garage,' he said, 'and the yard's a sheet of ice.'

I recall I said quite calmly, 'We'll take it slowly. Get the car out.'

He looked at me and said, 'Don't you realise I can hardly see a hand before my face.'

'All right; I'll sit it out,' I said.

But when, at six forty-five there was no let up, he saw he would have to risk it.

It took us an hour and a half to get to the roadworks approaching Newcastle. And there we joined a hold-up. I was feeling rather weak now but still quite calm, and we sat there for three-quarters of an hour moving but an inch at a time.

When at last we reached the Freeman Hospital, where Mr Marshall would now be at work, the time was half-past nine. The usual forty-five-minute journey had taken us two and three-quarter hours.

I was in a bit of a mess, having started bleeding at six o'clock, but somewhere along the journey thankfully it had clogged itself up. However, in the cleaning-up process it started to bleed heavily again, so making cauterisation difficult, and Hugo decided I must stay in hospital, which surprisingly did not engender in me any feeling of panic or dismay.

Not that I usually panic on such occasions, I'm so used to them, but I very often feel so ill that at times I ask myself if it is worth struggling on. Then I think of Tom, and the answer is as always. But on this morning I was still feeling utterly peaceful.

The irritating part of this particular complaint is, it takes no heed of either time or place, it gives no warning, except that I know it will erupt if I indulge in a good laugh or a good relieving bout of crying.

For four days I lived in this wonderful state of peace, and it would be good to say that it remained with me. It didn't; but the actual fact that it happened has; and, also, the comforting knowledge that I am afraid of Him no longer, that we can talk, He and I, plainly, of denominations and sects, and of the fallacies and perversions of the truth with regard to His life.

Anyway, my last words on the subject are, if it wasn't a miracle, it was the nearest thing I'll ever get to one. As it wasn't the result of faith, nor of reasoning, perhaps it was the answer to that which, in this age, is a belittled and ridiculed prayer, 'Gentle Jesus, meek and mild, look upon this little child.'

I can never picture Him being meek or mild, but I can see Him taking the hand of a much bewildered and hurt little child, once known under the name of Katie McMullen and who still exists just beneath the skin of Catherine Cookson.

Another Odd Happening

During our first months of evacuation to St Albans, I felt ill and yet deliriously happy: life was like a fairy tale, 'and they lived happy ever after'; I knew that whatever might happen our love could surmount it; and it surmounted the loss of my first baby on 6 December that year, after nine days in labour. I wouldn't go into hospital because I didn't want to be parted from Tom, and London was under siege: the bombs were dropping thick and fast every night, and so I felt if it was our turn next we should be together.

After the loss of the baby my recovery was slow, and it was some time in January before I was on my feet again. Our flat was small but it had two good-sized rooms and a smallish kitchen-cum-dining room and a bathroom. But there was no central heating and only a tiny fireplace in the kitchen.

It was some time in February. The day was very cold and I was standing in the bathroom washing some flannels in the sink. My hands were in lovely soapy water but my legs and feet were freezing, so I decided to go and bring in the electric fire from the kitchen.

This particular article had been bought in a second-hand shop after we acquired the flat. I think it must have been one of the first of its kind. The metal reflector was in shape the concave section of a sphere, about fourteen inches in diameter, with a cone of wire about four to five inches long as the heating unit. It stood on four iron feet and the handle was made up of a five-inch bar of twisted metal.

Anyway it fitted the hand and it fitted my soapy one. I let out a terrible scream as the electric current tore through me, which was to re-echo in my mind for many weeks. I was standing with it hanging from my hand, the cone a few inches from my dress. Terry, my little fox terrier, was jumping madly around me as I screamed.

I don't know how long it took for it to burn my hand dry, I only know that I got to the bottom of the stairs and managed to open the door before sliding down over the step and on to the pavement.

Fortunately, our little flat was next to a barber's shop and on the main road and right opposite the police station where a policeman was always standing outside on duty. It was war time and this was done then.

The next I remember was waking up in bed with the screams tearing through my head. My mouth was opening and shutting but no sound was emerging, but the screaming inside had not abated. The room seemed full of people.

What had transpired was that the policeman, with some help, had carried me upstairs, only to find that the kitchen was on fire. The electric fire had dropped from my hand on to the mat, and that was well alight. Tom, who was at school, and a doctor, who fortunately lived just across the road, had been sent for, and the latter put me to sleep.

Some time later, when I awoke, I was still

screaming in my head. Tom was sitting by my side, saying, 'It's all right, dear. It's all right. You'll be all right.'

I was feeling I would never be all right in my life again, for the screaming would never stop, and it didn't stop for days. It must have been a full month before I could pass a night when I didn't wake up hearing myself screaming.

There's an object lesson here: never buy second-hand electric goods.

Why had I bought such an object in the first place, I who am so particular? Why hadn't I had the sense to dry my hands before I picked it up, I who was so sensible?

And why did all these things seem to happen to me?

Anyway, came the spring and I felt I must get out and walk: go into the country, hear the birds.

Tom was very interested in birds, as was Alan, one of his school colleagues, and he suggested to Tom a nice walk, not too far from the town, where he would likely come across certain birds. He told Tom a particular by-road out of the town led to a main road and a bus route: not too far a walk for me to take, he said.

So it was on this April evening, about six o'clock, that we set out for what Tom called a gentle dander. It was a very nice by-road, very rural, and after we had been walking about fifteen minutes we came into a village or large hamlet. Beyond what appeared to be an inn was obviously a quarry. It was very quaint.

Because I was beginning to feel tired, I suggested

we get the bus back, and so we turned into what appeared to be a long main street.

Here we enquired of a man the time of the next bus back to St Albans.

The man peered at us and muttered, 'Bus?' then shook his head and walked on. And so did we for a little way further where we stopped to question a woman. She, too, looked puzzled before, pointing to what looked like an alley, she said, 'To the road.' We took the alley-way which led into a cart-track lane.

How far, hanging on to Tom, I walked I did not know, but we gasped with relief when we saw what looked like a large farmhouse. But there we found no-one about, and our knocking on the door brought no response; so again we walked on, and again we came to another large house, a farmhouse. It looked a more grand affair and there certainly were people about.

When Tom enquired of a man how to get to the main road, as we had lost our way, he shook his head and pointed across some fields and said briefly, 'No road round but straight across;' then he added rather sternly, 'You are on private land, but go.'

We went. How many fields we crossed I cannot remember, I only know I felt near to collapsing. Then suddenly Tom exclaimed, 'There's a railing.'

I had to bend double to get between the bars, and rolled straight into a ditch.

Tom pulled me out and sat me on the grass verge of what must have been the main road.

Alan had said it was only a fifteen-minute walk or so after leaving the town; but now it was getting dusk.

To cap everything, I began to bleed. Then, as welcome as the oasis in a desert, we saw a bus approaching.

The driver drew up, then kindly helped Tom to get me up the steps and into it. Fortunately, it was empty: there was no-one there to question whether or not I was drunk.

How I got back from that bus to my bed I'll never know, but I was there again, and for a good many days.

We had left the house just after six and in broad daylight; when we returned it was almost dark, although double summer-time had been introduced. Where had we been?

The following day Tom spoke of the place to Alan, who looked at him blankly, then said, 'There's no inn on that road, or quarry, or farm. Are you sure you followed the by-road?'

Tom was sure. He was also sure, when he enquired of a number of other people regarding the village, that they thought he had gone a little odd. An inn by a quarry and an endless village street and miles of farm land? Well, there must have been miles of it, mustn't there, when it took us so long to get across the fields?

Tom resorted to the map. There was no such village or hamlet dotted on it.

At last Tom stopped enquiring about the where-abouts of this place that people didn't think existed, and so we just talked about it and asked ourselves where then had we been that evening, and decided that when I was fit enough we'd go along that side road again, but that we'd turn back once we arrived at that inn. Yet even as we said this we both felt we wouldn't find an inn or a village or any fields. Something must have happened to us that night. What, we didn't know.

I was glad we could say *we* didn't know, for if the experience had been mine alone, the explanation would have been: Hysteria, my dear. Well, losing the baby and then practically electrocuting herself. Hysteria all right.

But there was Tom the mathematician, the sceptic. What about him?

I think he was a bit shaken by the whole experience. Did it or did it not happen? Did we not go through that place? Did we dream it? Then if we did, where were we during those hours it took us to dream it?

Some weeks later we walked up the side road again, and within fifteen minutes, as Tom's colleague had said, we came to the main road.

What had happened to us on that night and why? Why were we taken into that village, for village or hamlet it was? Did we enter a time warp? One thing we do know: we were both shaken by the experience, for nothing that had happened in either of our lives and has happened since seems to have had any connection with it.

However, I do know this: we attract atmosphere. That's the only way I can put it. Many years later we were to discover this on our trips up and down the Fenland rivers in our cabin cruiser, the *Mary Ann Shaughnessy*.

Thoughts in the Eighties

For me there is no future; just one day at a time and what spare time I have I spend looking back into the past, reliving it, analysing it, but without pain because one is not experiencing it. But the future: well, I know nothing about the future. I only know if I had to go by the age of my mind, which is still in its thirties, I could go on for say 'x' number of years. But then there is this body that is rotten from the eyebrows downwards. Yet isn't it strange that the only good thing in it is, supposedly, the heart? David, my doctor, is always saying, 'Damn it! woman, you have the blood pressure of a young woman and a heart as strong as a horse.' Well, I suppose I had to have something to sustain all the defects that at times drive me daft. Yet why, I ask, put a good engine in a leaking craft? It makes you think.

Later on, in July 1990, the engine didn't pass its MOT.

Don't laugh: I've had two heart attacks and three teeny ones. 'A heart as strong as a horse!' Yes, that of an old nag put out to grass.

The Heart

The heart is depicted as a centre of love,
This muscle that is but a pump for the
    blood:
My heart is breaking,
My heart is sad,
My heart is glad,
My heart is full
Of the joy of Spring,
Ring a ding ding,
Ring a ding ding.
And to all these sayings we firmly cling.
With palm pressed hard on to our chest
We beg our aching heart to rest.
But from where do we beg it?
Only from the brain, by which we really do
    exist;
For all the joy,
The pain, the ache,
Comes not from that muscle
Below the chest
But from that piece of matter up there,
Encased in bone.

. . . But wait!
Why yammer on thus?
For it's got to have a place

From which it can express
What impinges on it.
Without the sun
There'd be no light,
Without the night
Sleep would not come,
So without that drum
Beneath my chest
My brain, I fear,
Would remain dumb.

The North-east

The evening of 20 March 1974, I stood on the platform in the lovely theatre of the Technical College in South Shields and received from the Mayor the Freedom of the Borough.

That was a moment I shall never forget. Behind me sat the aldermen and councillors. In front of me was a packed hall, the first row taken up by 'me ain folk', Tom's face shining out from the rest, the pride in his eyes misting my own.

I had to speak for ten minutes. I made them laugh and when I cried they cried with me.

They were seeing Katie McMullen from 10 William Black Street, East Jarrow, who had walked the Jarrow road with the grey hen, or with the parcels for the pawn, or with a sack on her back as she followed the coke carts.

They were seeing Katie McMullen who had left the North never to return, only to find in after years that she had to go back and pick up her heart because she had left it there.

They were not seeing Catherine Cookson, the successful author, being honoured in her lifetime by the citizens of her home town – a prophet being honoured in his own country, which was something in itself – but Katie McMullen, because it was in Katie McMullen that the dreams had been born. It was in Katie McMullen that they struggled for thirty-four years.

A lot can happen during that time; and much had happened in Jarrow. Gone were great sections of the town I once knew; what had been the oldest part was now the newest. A Viking statue dominates the modern shopping centre. The structures left standing here and there on its outskirts are the only evidence that it has been built on ruins of the old . . . And the car park. Who in Jarrow could have afforded a car before the war! And the new estates, houses with indoor water, bathrooms and sanitation; gardens, blocks of flats; not to mention the new factories.

When I talk to those of my own generation they mostly say, at least the males do, 'By-aye! . . . aye, it's changed; it's grand!' Then a look comes into the eyes of some of them and they add, 'But, you know, something's gone. It might have looked mucky years ago but the houses were few and far between, those that were mucky inside; she had to be a real dirty bitch to let her house go. An' I tell you what I miss, Pet, the closeness, the mateyness.'

If I'm talking to a woman, she's likely more voluble. 'Oh, there's no comparison, lass; central heating, a fridge, and . . . the greatest benefit man has given to woman, the washing machine. Eeh! the washing in our day: poss tub and wringer. And then there's the freedom: we're no longer under their thumbs. Why, me da never took me ma out, not once in all their married life. But I can tell you things are different now: mine takes me to the social club three times a week. I say he takes me, 'cos you can only go as a man's guest. An' that's the last link in the chain of the men's domination . . . the clubs are still classed as men's clubs, you see. When that rule's broken it'll be equality at last. And no class distinction anywhere. Well, class distinction's finished, isn't it?'

I wonder. No class distinction? Then why do the supposed white-collar workers have their own type of clubs instead of being members of the social clubs? And why have the . . . ? Oh, one could go on and on; then come to the conclusion that there still exists a class distinction as finely drawn as in the old days when the station stairs separated the lower from the upper part of the town.

Yet, I must say there has been a breakthrough, and the young have done it. The young of 1974 are a different species, they can mix. They do mix. Now that one's mother doesn't have to do for the others, they spread out. They mingle in night clubs, physics labs, and concert halls from Sunderland to Newcastle; and they don't want to hear any more about the march of the empty-bellied men from their town to London in 1936. They rear, and rightly, when it is said Shields has its technical college, Newcastle its university and Jarrow its march. They resent the fact that the march has brought Jarrow to the notice of the nation more than has the Father of Learning, their own St Bede. No; the young are speaking. Gone is the admonition 'Speak when you are spoken to'. They have spread beyond the precincts of their backyards. The Tyne and all on it is theirs. Newcastle University is theirs. They use it, sing its praises, criticise it, but damn any outsider who dares to speak one word against it.

They are a unique breed, the people who are bred

on the banks of the River Tyne, they are linked as by one family tie, yet so individual in their loves and hates, their narrowness, their bigotry; they still wear the thongs that bind them to the past with pride, the past from which their forebears have struggled to lift them to the frontier of the present. Their views still remain narrow insomuch as they desire the security of a home place, a womb, and the womb is the North-east.

Lonely

I am lonely behind my smile:
I feel desperate most of the time,
Especially in the night;
So I turn to my soul and plead
To show me the way to fill this need,
Not to suggest I follow the dogmatic gods
Presented by good people who insist they
    know
Their road is the way I should go;
I want a path that is wide and clear,
Swept free of all fear.

I wait,
And my soul replies,
There are laws you must learn.
You have from the dawn to the night in
    which to call a truce
And stop the constant fight of asking why,
For there's no answer to that question, no
    matter how you try.
So let your heart smile as well as your face,
Use the wisdom you have gained,
Stop wasting your days
And remember the race of life is but a
    space,
A mere tick allotted to the human race.

Age 11

When needs are diminishing, if not already
    unnecessary,
And life is something that has been used,
Worn and sold to the past
For a price, the receipts written
In fadeless memories,
Recriminations against time and fate
Are too late to alter now.

What a pity that the agony of age
Does not penetrate our minds in youth,
Facing us with the truth
That we are but a flicker in time.
Yet would we hear the voice of age
At that stage?
No; and rightly so.
Life whether long or short
Is ours to travel to the end,
In wealth or poverty,
In humbleness or pride,
And there pay the price for the ride.

A Few More Crosses

It is 28 May 1984 and I've just heard on the radio that Eric Morecambe died yesterday, died on the job, as it were, collapsing after he came off stage. I wonder what Ernie Wise is feeling at this moment; their partnership must have been like a marriage all these years.

Some people say, it's the best way to go, in harness. I don't know. If you're afraid of death, yes; if you're not, I think I'd prefer the approach to it to be slow and, if possible, painless, so one could think about it and prepare for it. That, of course, as I said, is if you're not afraid of it . . . and who, deep in his heart, isn't afraid of it?

It's a very odd thing; we really don't know anything about it, perhaps not even those who have suddenly found themselves close to it, as I imagined I was one day last week after a further violent haemorrhage.

However, I was given some assurance by Hugo, Mr Marshall, my specialist. He told me of a patient who had died two years previously at ninety years of age. He used to refer to her as 'the other one of you I have in hospital'. And when she died he said she hadn't died from telangiectasia, simply from old age, and that when she had come on to his books fourteen years previously, she was then seventy-six and by her records she'd already had six hundred pints of blood pumped into her, and from the time she came under his care had a transfusion every three weeks.

So, following this, I had to ask myself what I was worrying about, yet ten heavy haemorrhages in two months, not counting the little ones, was knocking the stuffing out of me.

But after some quiet reflection I thought of the good points still applying to me: I could still walk, I could still talk, I could still see, but above all I had a *mind* and therein had power over all my minor miseries.

But thinking of that old girl again living till she was ninety, coming next Friday 1 June, I shall be only seventy-eight. I have another twelve years to catch up to her. Oh, Lord! what a prospect, especially if He deigns to add a few more crosses . . . He wouldn't do it, would He?

You never know.

The Question I

Are these ills in my body alone?
Is not my soul the instigator of this pain
From my limbs to my brain?
Yet is not my brain the interpreter
Which opens up the channel of the notion
That I have the will to conquer?
I have but to say *I will*,
And in my case it will be done.

The 'I' in me is large,
It expands awareness to the knowledge of self;
But I am wise in that I know I count as
      nothing
And would be but a hollow shell were it not
      for love.
I am surrounded by love,
Washed by its great waves,
Ocean rollers sweeping over me
From all the seas of humankind.
So why do I remain immune to its power to
      heal me?

Why does the core of my being remain cold?
Except towards that one,
For he cannot be counted in the throng;
He has been within my being so long.

He was in the beginning . . .
Not just since the marriage bed;
And will be there to the end.
After, who knows?

But again I ask,
From where comes my pain?
From the spirit which is called my soul?
Or is the soul and body one whole,
Obedient to the brain?
But does it matter?
Why do I strain?
What can I gain?
The pain is with me:
Prayers and love are of no avail;
Haven't I said my life
Is built on strife, body, soul, and brain?
So be it.

The Need

*(written after reading a distressing letter from
a reader)*

Kiss me;
Not just on the cheek.
Hold me tight;
As if I were weak,
Frail.
Sit close;
Hold my hand;
Stroke my fingers,
Silently telling me you understand
The need of love
That you cannot transmit
With your perfunctory peck.

But there you sit,
Perusing yet another page.
If only you'd raise your head
And ask, 'All right, dear?'
Or look at me,
As if I were a need,
At least of some sort.
Yet you are aware of my presence,
Which is the last blow of devastation to
    my pride;

And with it I am brought low
When, from behind the unruffled page
Your voice, in no shout,

But calm and thin,
Says, 'What is wrong with you?
Why don't you read a book!'
Dear God above!
I do not wish I were dead,
I only know that tomorrow
I will secretly sin once more
To erase the pain yet again,
Because I need love.
Oh, how I need love!

The Community

God gnashed the earth with His teeth,
And chewed up slate, rock and shale;
Then spat out green segments
To cover the scarred ridges,
And named the bite a dale.

Then He dug His heel into the depth
To initiate His opponent's hell,
Where blackness reigned so deep
That eyes were without sight,
And stillness cried aloud
And begged a spoken word
To shatter the man's bond sealed in writ,
And to this hole He gave
The name of pit.

And to this place He guided men
And dropped them to the depth,
Where like animals they crawled,
Each one in himself alone,
His flesh naked to the stone,
At which he hacked as if in flight
From that depth that showed eternal night.

And for this thing called coal,
What was his reward

For bringing it to the light?
Blue marks on skin,
Blackened body and dust within
And a cough that racked the night.

But there was a prize,
God was not unkind;
He doled out a privilege which entwined
Families in loyalty to their kind;
Marras in blood, sweat and song,
They tillaged;
And they called it a pit village.

1984 – The Pondering Year

It is 17 March 1984. I have had a very bad week with bronchitis and laryngitis, and four bleedings within nine days. Last Saturday saw me at rock bottom; I felt I was for pneumonia and the hospital. But here I am, coming up out of the depths again, although it is a slow crawling business.

How on earth do I survive these things? As I look back at my life over the years, I seem always to have been fighting to survive, fighting to throw off my back the people who had latched on to me, fighting the vascular trouble I inherited, and this coupled with anaemia. Even the fall in the school yard when I was thirteen has its repercussions to this day, causing me to have to lie on a board. Then I must say that I am not asking the question how I survived out of any feeling of pity for myself, but I would like to know from where came the strength that has enabled me to still be here. It certainly isn't in my physical system, nor yet is it in my mind, because I am a fearful person – when I say fearful I mean fear-filled – so I can only think that the answer lies in the spirit, that intangible, elusive quality that cannot be claimed as part of one's character, but I think must be looked upon more as a gift, a gift of power, but not such that is singled out and donated to any special person, but is, as I have said elsewhere, a sort of universal gift – but a gift that needs to be used.

Then why doesn't everyone tap it? I don't know. I think perhaps you can only get in touch with it when, through extremity, anguish, or indeed innocence, your need becomes known. I've known extremity, I've known anguish, and, yes, I've known and dwelt in innocence, or shall I say I've wanted to dwell in innocence, inasmuch as I've wanted to be good. Yet I know, only too well, I've failed in this again and again. I don't consider I am what you call good, but I do consider in a very infinitesimal way, as is a grain of sand compared with a strand, that I have acquired some sort of wisdom that has enabled me to understand people, to see into them as it were. Yet, I ask myself, if I have gained wisdom then shouldn't I be kind in my thoughts to the objectionable traits I find in many people? If I have gained wisdom shouldn't I make allowances for their failures? If I have gained wisdom, why am I irritated by so many people? Why do I dissect them and condemn them for their way of life? Why, if I have gained wisdom, do I not just concentrate on the good in them?

Why? Why? Why?

In practical terms, such as the giving of money, it would seem I am generous, so why doesn't this grain of wisdom of mine control my thinking, at least embody it in a coat of softness? But it does, that is when I am trying to alter another's negative view. We each have a façade, behind which we hide. Mine is a tough façade hiding the fears of a very weak woman who would go under if it wasn't for that thing that led me into this piece of inward-looking talk, the spirit.

Almost every day I receive letters about my work when people tell me what they think about me, how they love me. So, what would happen if someone were to say to me, 'Isn't it wonderful to be cared for and loved by so many people?' Were I to speak the truth, I would have to say, 'I cannot take this in, for it means little to me.' And yet I am grateful to be told this.

But do I love these same people more? No; not as I think of love.

Well, what makes me think of love? First, looking at my husband; then at my dogs.

I cannot contemplate the loss of my husband, but I have already experienced the agony in losing a dog; and in this state I have known what real love is, in fact, what passionate love is.

Life has taught me it is not necessary to love people in order to feel their need. With humans, I think liking far exceeds love. If you can love and like at the same time then you have got something, but love on its own is merely a candle with a string wick; it will eventually die out. Liking is a strong iron candlestick upholding the wick; at least, this is as I see it through my little glimmer of wisdom.

Recompense

Let me forget
The hurts, the pain,
The despising, the shame,
The loneliness, the longing,
The needing to feel secure
And never to be sure . . .
Oh never to be sure . . .
Of my place in this span;

　　But,

Let me remember,
While climbing wearily this last hill,
All those good people
Who, over the years, and still,
Send me each day
Their kind words of appreciation
And, above all, love;
Faces I've never seen,
Hands I've never touched,
Tell me how much
I mean to them,
How my words
Have lightened their days,
Helped them to stand and face
Life's tortuous ways;

Made them laugh and cry;
But, above all,
Made them ponder.

So,

Let me think of these:
My dear friends
Who have never come within my sight,
But who have given me the answer
To why I have been given
My place in this span,
Which is to write.

The Clasp

I was in a station,
Waterloo.
I saw two lovers leave a train.
Separate, they walked towards me,
Went past, and on again,
Both tall and straight and beautiful,
Their eyes shining in love's first youth;
Then shyly their fingers touched and
     clasped.

Who were they?
Whence did they come?
Whither did they go?
To what future I do not know,
I only know, on that day my heart sang
And I was touched as if by a spray
From the fountain of their love,
And the pages of my life rolled away
And I was sixty no more
But young and gay,
Walking straight through Waterloo
After meeting the train and you.

Counting Your Chickens

The morning was bright,
My spirits were light;
I'd been at my desk since just after dawn.
The feeling of being tired and worn
Had lifted.
My hospital second sojourn
Was four days past;
I was coming up for air.
Moreover, in three weeks' time
I'd have gone a full half year
Without needing specialised blood care.
Wonderful! to feel alive:
No allergy, no pain,
In fact I was young again.
And after breakfast I would dress and plan
    my day,
And look forward to the mail,
Phone calls,
Checking scripts,
And the oddments, come what may.

Why have I never learned
That the gods are in control
Of my being as a whole,
That I must never plan
Or think ahead?

They have warned me time and again
That the only thing of which I can be sure
Is that some day I'll be on the other shore.
And they proved it yet again
When my nose exploded in a gush;
And before I had time to cry, 'No! No!'
Tom had proceedings under way,
Hieing me to Newcastle in my nightgown
    and bedsocks still,
With, topping all, a fur hood,
A real sight to see!
Finished off in blood.

Why . . . why does it happen to me?
No, it isn't through self-pity I seek to know,
And I'm past the answer religion might give
To show that the Christian God
Tests those he loves,
For to that I'd say
'Like hell He does.'

There must be a reason why,
Even at eighty-two, my life
Continues to be a fight.

Oh! don't say
It's because it gives me material with which
    to write,
And the insight into pain;
And, moreover, look what it's brought me:
Position and wealth.
Well, let me tell you; anyone may have it all
In exchange for only one year of health.

Growing

I think, I ponder, I meditate.
My mind rakes the ages
And clutches with greedy hands
The pearls dropped by the sages.
In the diffused light of dreams
I see them as chips
Chopped off the rock of universal
    thought,
Diamond bright,
In lightning flashes of memory,
Eons old, before the earth cooled.
And I drag them back
Through the mind of time,
Holding fast in the dream
Until the beam of consciousness
Splinters the magic thought of knowing.
And I awake once more
To think, to ponder, to meditate
In the painful process of growing.

Time

Where has the day gone?
Where has the month gone?
Where has the year gone?
Why is time escaping from my life,
Now in the last span
When strife should be but a memory
And days soothed with calm-filled ease,
And the short future
A blessed space to do as I please,
Ruminate or contemplate
And rest smugly in a job well done;
Even now and again have fun . . .
Just a little,
And of a quiet kind,
Made up of mirth and wit,
Pleasures of the mind.

BUT WHAT HAPPENS?

Each hour of each day
Is filled with work:
Writing, writing, letters, scripts,
This and that;
And then the phone . . .
Not for small talk and chat,
But down to business

That eats and gollops precious time.

But pause here and think:
If your hour was as a long day,
And a day seemed never ending,
And you could sit at ease and ruminate,
No hurry, flurry,
How long do you think you would last?
Long enough to write
Your own obituary.

Time is long
Only to the bored
And the lonely.

Knowledge I

You imagine there is nothing
They cannot explain;
And that all will be your gain
If you but follow their thought
Over their lifetime dearly bought;
And so you plough
Through chapters of know-how:
Plato, Aristotle, Descartes and Kant.
On and on through them you go,
Until you become aware
Each of them rants on
What he alone knows . . .

. . . But knows what?

Wearily I go back
Down the centuries to Socrates
Speaking with simplicity to his last
    breath
While awaiting the poison cup
That will deliver him to death,
And thankfully I struggle
Out of the knowledge trance
And translate his thought to my own:
I know nothing;
I'm only aware of my ignorance.

But how comforting are his words,
At least to me, and kind,
After the struggle to understand
The lords of the mind.

It

There you are now. Come on; sit up!
The nurse said.
Have you had a good night?

Did I have a good night?
A good night looking back
Through burning eyes at the past
Wherein was bred the searing desire to know
About IT,
To experience . . . IT,
The IT that had not to be spoken of,
Not in our house, anyway.

My mother stands by the bed
In the buzzing ward
And mutters yet again,
I warned you.
Dear God! I made it plain.
It's insane, you are, girl . . . insane.
Your Dad will never have you back again.
You know what he's like:
He still believes it's a sin.
Well! I must away.
If I can't get in tomorrow
Someone will come.
Likely Our Pat;

234

You know what Sunday's like,
With the dinner and all that.

Oh yes, I know what Sunday is like,
With the dinner and all that.
Why can't one love one's people?
The only thing to love in that house
Was the cat.
And yet she too was full of disdain.
Love could only be achieved by IT . . .
That IT again.
My mother's parting words were,
Think about what you're going to do with IT.

And here IT comes,
The IT
That was created
From ignorance and curiosity about
The REAL IT.

I hold her and look down into her crumpled
      face,
And fearfully and strangely there pierces me,
Like a knife in my heart,
The fact that she is part of me;
And stranger still,
I swear by my father's God, which I hate,
That fate won't bring her to my state;
And in that maleless room, somewhere,
One thing I vow will shine,
For, if nothing else,
She will know love
And that she is mine.

I wrote the above in 1967.

Looking back I have my granny and step-grandfather to thank for so much. They gave me love, which gift I didn't realise until in middle age I began to recall my childhood. My grandmother's love ceased when I was eight; she died. But my grandfather's love followed me when I left the North at twenty-two. When, a year later, he, too, died, I saw that he was buried decently with the money I'd been saving for his funeral since I was eighteen, all of twenty pounds. It was little enough payment, for love.

The Accepted Mystery

What is sleep?
Describe it to me.
Don't just wipe it off by saying
It's the forerunner of death,
For with death we lose our breath.

I go through the process:
I watch my eyelids close;
I imagine I'm in repose
And see my mind
Sink from its level
Into the depths of its other life.
There I lie on the crest of gentle waves
In soft folding seas
Before I race the clouds,
Then topple into their billowing froth,
To drop . . . to drop . . . to drop,
Into blackness now,
Like hell.
And although I yell and yell,
It is but a whisper
That I alone can hear.
The words my granny said,
If you wake before you touch the bottom
You will not be dead,
Comfort me.

I walk into a green meadow:
My shadow is long
Before it shrinks into a child
Laughing in my arms,
Knowing the while
I had given birth
And my life had been of worth,
But why do I cry?

I'm in blackness again,
Being dragged back
On to the mind's other plane.
I lift my lids:
My face is wet with tears.
In sleep
I've had what they term a dream;
Sleep is but a part of life it would seem.
That's no answer.

My Hands

I bless my hands
As I look at them today:
They are bony, wrinkled, mottled and old;
But they have served me well:
They have scrubbed and rubbed,
They have hoed and raked,
They have felled and sawn,
Until the tips were worn;
They have been made to work like no hands
     should,
They have worked ceaseless hours in the day,
And in the dark hours drew from my mind
Words that escape the light of reasoning day.

What duty they evinced was dead to me,
Yet strangely this quality others could see,
Until now, amazed, I find
They are to be hung in the Academy.
To look at them now
I have to hold them close to my eyes
For I can no longer see,
Yet I join them and bless them
These wrinkled, blue-veined bony hands
Which have served me so faithfully.

Philosophy

There I was reading some philosophy when I realised I was, at the same time, working out how I would alter that piece to simplify it. Most writing on philosophy is much too wordy. It defeats itself in its purpose.

I stopped suddenly and, looking at the page, I asked myself if I could remember what I had read while at the same time my mind was going off at the above tangent. And yes, I could; at least I had the substance of it.

And there was a third thing. Not only was I reading that paragraph, not only was it being interjected by thoughts of what I meant to do by way of simplifying it, but on a third plane my mind was making me aware of the previous two instances. All this, I imagined, had happened instantly; but then it could have happened in a matter of seconds; or again there could have been a greater time lapse. I don't know. I only know that the mind is an amazing instrument over which, in spite of free will, I have really little control.

I was very interested to read that Plato stresses this fact. I don't know whether or not he was reiterating the views put over by Socrates when he states that we are born already with a terrific amount of knowledge and that much of what we think we learn in life has simply resulted from our delving into the storehouse that was already there. I firmly believe this because why other can a child sit down at the piano and compose a sonata when he has just begun to learn to walk and talk? Child prodigies, as they are called.

I think that, unless the brain is damaged in some way by a defect of the body in which it first grew, or by the effects of man's handiwork in distorting nature's natural gifts through indulgence in drugs, then in all of us there is the power, more or less, along one channel or another to bring over from that mysterious watery realm of being before birth some talent, and that whatever has supplied this store of knowledge in the first place has given each of us a life to work it out.

A fancy?

No. I recognise it all around me and particularly within myself.

Socrates said that no-one does wrong willingly. Well, that is pooh-poohed today, as it was in his own day. He wants to say that it is because of lack of knowledge that we do wrong. I interpret that as, if a person has been brought up well and given good examples he will resist evil. Well, in my own life I've found that to be a myth and to know that there are many forms of evil, ranging from the physical to the mental.

Socrates never wrote down a word; it was left to Plato to record him, as it was with Jesus and the writers of the Gospels. It is odd that it was not Jesus but Paul who laid the foundations for the Church. Never having experienced anything of Jesus's life whilst he lived, he set up what is now taught as the Christian religion. What Jesus preached was passed on by word of mouth, and we all know that can change from tongue to tongue. The precept might remain but the writer's view of the spoken word is naturally translated through his own thoughts.

Nothing much changes in that way. Someone tells us something; if we pass it on, or when we pass it on, and we have a sense of humour, the message is threaded with our own particular thought. Or, on the other hand, if we are of a vicious turn of mind the original words can be so arranged that the meaning spurts vitriol.

What amazes me about philosophy is that Plato, between the years 447 and 427 BC, continued to puzzle over the meaning of love, and in doing so revealed a point so relevant to humanity in all ages, which is that as the years grow on us so do our ideas change.

He had been a devout student of Socrates whose messages he wrote down and whose views he followed until his middle years. Then, like many of us, he started to think for himself, and from then on some of his ideas contradicted those of Socrates about which he had written. Then, in his later writings he simplifies the most intricate thinking and states that it isn't so much the answers that matter but what we think and dig from our own minds in the process of finding out.

With regard to the word answer, it would appear that when one philosopher finds the answer to his particular problem or search, another comes up and dissects it and off we go again, tearing apart, probing, dissertating. It's never-ending. Right up to this present time.

A few years ago, on TV, in a series dealing with philosophy and philosophers, the interviewer was Bryan Magee; and I came to the conclusion that here was a man I could listen to and learn from: he simplified the high-falutin' jargon that cripples the word 'philosophy'.

The Salve of Life

Say, I love you.
Go on, say it aloud.
Say, I need you.
Go on, don't be too proud.
Tell him . . . or her
They are a being apart,
Special . . . different.
You knew it from the start.
Get into the habit:
Do it every day;
It'll catch on,
Then hopefully come to stay.
And the dividend will be surprising:
A hundred per cent, I promise you,
On what you pay
For this salve of life
You give
To either
Your man or your wife.

Wishing

I wanted to be a film star,
I wanted a mink coat,
I wanted a BMW and a yacht,
And a romantic Frenchman or Swede or
    German,
And look what I got:

Tommy Rafferty!
And what did he give me?
The back seat at the Odeon
And kids,
Not one,
Not two,
But seven.
And he tells me his aim is eleven!

So much for a film star, a mink coat, a
    BMW and a yacht,
A romantic Frenchman,
Or Swede,
Or German.
Mon Dieu!
Mitt Gud!
Mein Gott!

The Inevitable

There's a battle you cannot win,
And that's the battle against the skin.
You can cream and lotion and pat,
But it's triumphant in the end.
I know that.
The only compensation is the neck.
Strangely, you can conquer that:
Rid it of chollops and its chins;
Only remember that the fight begins
When you first attack your face.
Pay it as much attention then,
And when
The battle against age is won
And bags hang down,
Lines criss-crossed and fine,
You'll find
The skin below the chin has held,
And can be viewed
Without a hopeless frown
If you remember:
Never stroke it up, always stroke it down.

With Apologies to Louis Armstrong

What a wonderful world
To see pen and ink and pencils too,
Paper by the ream, all waiting for you.

What a wonderful world
In which to have thoughts that flow
Down from your brain to your fingers
   below,
To take your pen and transfer to the page
Characters of people from youth to age.

What a wonderful world
In which to apply an art
Of telling a story right from the start
Through love and devotion and sadness and
   fear
That will extract from a reader a smile or a
   tear.

What a wonderful world
To experience and know
You've been given a talent in which to show
You owe a debt to the gifts you possess
By working at them each day, more or less,
For all are numbered for your span.
Just tell yourself you will and you can,

And if you hadn't realised it before,
Who knows? You might live to a hundred
     and four.
By! My! 'Tis a wonderful world.

PS. Strange, I must have felt happy that morning
listening to the radio.

Pimms No. 1

They had never touched wine
Until one Saturday night
When we and they were taken out to
    dine.
I didn't know they were TT,
No-one had told me
Or them
That Pimms No. 1 was not all fruit.

After three, they refused wine and said
They'd stick to the tall glasses;
That'd be fine.
Another one, and they were far gone,
Three sheets in the wind,
All sails set.

Laugh? We laughed till we cried
To see the antics of those two:
He the new parson and she his mate,
Who, the following morning, would have
    a date
In the pulpit of St Mike's.

And what was the last straw?
They had come on their bikes.

The Angel's Wing

I tried to pick a sunbeam off the mat.
Did you ever hear of such a silly thing as that,
Trying to pick a sunbeam off a mat?
It was lying there so soft and bright
In the early morning light.
I didn't remember dropping anything last
    night.

My head was muzzy, I hadn't slept;
There had been times in the night when I
    think I wept;
But I stooped to pick up this bright thing off
    the mat,
And when the light fell on my fingers
I lingered open-mouthed for a space
While a smile spread o'er my face;
And the day became bright
And my heart began to sing
As I whimsically thought
I'd tried to pick up the dust of an angel's wing.

As the Americans Say

Have a nice day,

Or if you don't, stick it out,
There's always tomorrow.

What are you saying?
There'll be no tomorrow for many of us,
There's only now, this minute, or perhaps
    this day.

All right, all right, it may be as you say:
You, I, and a few more will be on our
    way.
But as we don't know as to what, where,
    or how,
There's only now,
So let's have a nice day.

The dawn is breaking.
I look at the light
Forcing its way through the curtains,
And to the gods that be, I say,
Make this a happy day;
Just for once don't let anything jar it,
Or mar it,
Or worse, cross swords with words,

Or be upset by what the reviewers say;
Just for once let everything be harmonious
    this day,
A day running on wheels
Oiled with smiles;
Let me love people
Like I love dumb creatures.
Oh, just for once let it be a joyful day.
Come what may, let me laugh
And want to dance, skip and prance,
Even though I know I can't, at this stage of
    my age.
But there's nothing to stop me letting my
    hair down,
Metaphorically, say.
So do
Let's have a nice day,
As the Americans say.

Cinders and Her Prince

(Written in my teens when I thought I had realised
the futility of the Cinderella dream. Strangely, it did
come true, didn't it?)

If horses could talk
And pigs could fly
And dogs could sing a lullaby,
Then you and I,
Hand in hand,
Would dance before the village band,
And together for ever
Live in a hut.
But . . . But . . .
But . . . But . . .
Horses can't talk
And pigs can't fly
And there's nobody . . . nobody . . .
Nobody . . . nobody . . .
Who'd listen to a dog
Singing a lullaby,
So, hand in hand,
We will not go
And before the village band show
Our prowess in the dance.
As for the hut,
Into that you would not go.

Oh no . . . Oh no . . .
Oh no . . . Oh no,
For where would you put
Your butler, footman and your maid?
As for the canopied bed,
Oh dear . . . Oh dear . . .
All has been said.
All has been said:
You and I can never wed.

The Impossible

On 1 January 1993 I was made a Dame; I also received a beautiful basket of flowers with a hand-written letter; and I cried.

Oh, I cried and I cried. And Katie McMullen from 10 William Black Street, East Jarrow, cried with me, for who, outside a fairy tale, could be so honoured by a Queen and a Prince in one day?

Dear Friend

'You've got a nice neck,' she said.
She never mentioned my face:
'You've got a nice neck,' she said,
'The skin is still in place;
For eighty-two,' she said, 'you're
Not bad, you're not bad at all.
But then, you've got no need to bother
At your age.'
She was again looking at my face . . .
No need at all.

Bella's Morning Prayer

The day is dull, O Lord,
The horizon darker still.
I need Your help to get through it, Lord;
Only of course if it is Thy will.
But if You could devise a way, Lord,
To make my lot understand
I'm right in what I say,
It would help to take the grey
From this dreary washing day.

You see, there's him, Lord.
I know it is a sin
This desire to kill off his pigeons
And to hope he doesn't win
On the pools or the horses
Or the dogs down at the course,
Or to potch him for moonlighting,
For that would bring remorse.
As he himself says, Lord,
It would empty half me purse.

And then there's our Delia, Lord,
Who you know is weak.
She never seems to seek trouble
But she's got a funny streak.

It's got her in the club again
And this is her third go.
As for the name of the bloke, Lord,
Well, she doesn't know.
Her da last night went barmy
And raised bloody . . . I mean the show.
Oh, she'll have to go, Lord. Oh, she'll have
    to go.

And then there's our Billy,
You know, the one that's big and tall.
You took a hand with him, Lord.
By! You did an' all,
Because now he just follows after lorries
In case anything should fall.

Yet his da keeps keeping on, Lord,
About him landing in the jug,
But as You know, Lord,
Billy is no mug:
Billy takes after me, Lord,
While his da hasn't much up top;
In fact, altogether, Lord,
He isn't much cop.

Ah! Here comes the sun, Lord,
To take away the grey.
You do do things, Lord,
In your own particular way,
Every now and then.
Let's hope I have a good drying day.

So for the present;
In the name of the Father
And of the Son
And the Holy Ghost,
AMEN.

Bob's Big Toe!

I was asked by the BBC to write an article for a booklet that was to complement the *In Touch* radio programme, which deals with the blind and the partially sighted. You might already have read it. But the dealings I had with the blind during the first years of the war would alone fill a book.

It should happen that I had left the laundry in 1939 to take over running my side business of a guest house. After much trauma my mother and my friend had gone their separate ways, and I was left with two mental patients and two male guests. Of the latter, one was a Captain Evans, the other, Mr Thomas Henry Cookson, the grammar-schoolmaster. He it was who had been a guest at my mother's house before she was forced to return to the North through her drinking and debts.

In one way, things were now, and at last, running smoothly for me. I was putting my house in order. I was a natural manager and I knew that I'd make a good business of it; then war broke out.

We won't go into blackouts and bustle et cetera, but the first real information that touched me was a letter to say that because I had this large house I had to take in twelve blind evacuee women from London. Believe it or not, Hastings had been designated as a reception area for evacuees.

Oh dear Lord, I remember saying to myself; what do I know about the blind? And twelve blind women! Where am I going to put them?

Well, it was either that or the house being taken over for the purpose.

Forgetting about the blackouts and a thousand and one other things one had to prepare for, we set about rearranging the bedrooms, the dining room and the drawing room . . . my drawing room, a room I loved. I put in more easy chairs and arranged flowers in the corners: if they couldn't see them very well they could smell them. It was a beautiful room that led into a small conservatory and I looked upon it as mine. It was the only place in which I could find rest after a twelve- to fourteen-hour day, and only when everyone else in the house had gone to bed.

The coach was due to arrive at five o'clock. Everything was ready. My one helper, Gladys, my deaf cook who could burn water, and Tom were waiting, probably with the excitement of the unknown; my feelings were more of apprehension; and so, when we heard the coach on the drive we rushed to the door. Then each one of us stood aghast as from it there was helped twelve blind men.

Suddenly coming alive, I said, 'They're not for here, I'm expecting twelve blind women. Please get them back!'

'Oh no, missis; the women have gone to some place else, and these have come from the East End of London and I'm not taking them back.'

The men were all turned towards me. They were a motley crowd: all except four seemed to have been sleeping in their clothes for ever. One man stood out.

He was in his fifties. He was very thin and he was wearing sand shoes, and sticking out of one of them was a big toe. There was no sock on the foot and the nail above the toe looked enormous. At the first glance it appeared to me like the end of a ram's horn.

I looked around. One was a very old man who was being supported by two others. This one became known as Old Daddy. The best dressed one of them was a different type of man, also in his fifties. He was supporting a tall young boy who was obviously totally blind. In utter dismay I turned about to go back into the house, and they all followed me.

We sat them in the hall and gave them a cup of tea the while I pondered on their bedrooms.

So began a very hard, eventful and educational year.

If, prior to this, I had been asked if I disliked blind people I would have gasped and emphasised nobody could dislike blind people. Pity them, sorry for them, but never dislike them. But up till then I'd had nothing to do with blind people, and so I was to learn quickly that they were just like the rest of humanity. Some you liked and some you didn't, and right from the first I didn't like Horace. He was the well-dressed one, who at one time had been sighted. He could now partially see and he had taken charge of Harold, a young boy of nineteen, and his influence over him was strong.

Then there was the eldest among them. He was on ninety and had to be carried upstairs and straight-away put to bed under a window, there to lie for the rest of his stay, and while being nursed, to grumble and yell and curse in very flowery language: he would begin talking quietly, mumbling the words, 'All through one man'; a pause, then somewhat louder, 'All through one man', rising to a crescendo (for a near ninety-year-old) 'All through one BLOODY man! Oh! God, why don't you TAKE ME?'

In the same bedroom we put Bob, the one with the big toe, and Little Daddy. Little Daddy was a charming man. He had a glimmer of light only, but he was so kindly and gentle with all the others. He was one of the three guests who had visitors from London during their stay. How the others might have lived or been cared for, I don't know; I could only surmise, in all probability roughly. But there was Bob, partially sighted and with that big toe.

Bob was a good fellow and a great help to me, but he became the bane of my life. I forgot to mention there was one woman. She had come with her husband; he was blind, not she. Oh no, she had all her sight and cockney wits, and she soon set out to use them. But we came to a quick understanding.

She would receive the dinners being passed through the hatch and would quietly nip off pieces of meat from other men's plates and direct them to those of her husband and her own.

Horace saw this, but like all starters he made the bullets for others to fire, and so Harold would complain that he had very little meat. From then on, Miss Mac, as they all called me, attended the dinner table, but she caused a lot of fun.

On the wireless (not the radio) at that time was a programme called *Monday Night At Eight*, and so I devised a Tuesday Night At Seven and gave them all a weekly do. We would invite a few friends who would dance with the men to the music of a gramophone. But little Mrs W. and Tom – my Tom – would cause gales of laughter by doing the Apache Dance. He was a small athletic young man, and she was smaller still, which was a good job because she allowed him to fling her across the well-polished floor as had happened in a film. How I managed it I don't know, but the evening would end with a glass of beer and a few fancy odds and ends.

I was allowed £1 a head, out of which I had not only to feed them, but, as the authoritative letter had implied, to clothe them if any of my friends could help in this way. As for washing the clothes, well, in those days – I was thirty-three and single – I couldn't afford to send all their odd undergear to a laundry, and, as some of it was indescribable, I couldn't handle it, so put it in the bath and stamped it clean.

I'll never forget the Monday morning when, weary and tired and not in any good mood, I was stamping away at some of these filthy flannels, the door opened and Gladys handed me a large pinky-brown envelope bearing a crest. Now I had always been particular about how I opened letters. In a last resort I would use a hair-pin to open them. But this morning I stood in that bath and I put my finger under what I imagined was another official demand of some kind, only to pull out a sort of parchment bearing Queen Elizabeth's signature. It was a letter thanking me for the work I was doing for the blind under such circumstances. Ungraciously, I handed it back to Gladys, saying, 'It would be more appropriate if she sent me a washing machine and a calender.' The calender, in this case, referred to the big four-roller machine in the laundry that would iron a sheet in its whole width once through it.

Anyway, I kept and still have the Queen's letter with its torn envelope, never thinking that one day I would receive another envelope, this time from her daughter, in fact two, but I had to live a long life before that was to happen.

My days were full from morn till night. I had still the two mental defectives under my care. Pansy the epileptic lay in the next bedroom to mine, and her fits would get me up half a dozen times a night. But one thing was, she stayed mostly in bed; not so Muriel. Muriel was upstairs in a very large attic room. She hated everyone, especially men, and she had anorexia; it was a job to get her to eat her meals or even anything else. You had to have eyes in the back of your head to watch Muriel. But she knew we had blind men in the house.

In 1939 it was feared that gas canisters might be used in air attacks and so the public was warned of this and issued with gas masks; also we were urged to make at least one room in the house gas-proof: stuffing wet paper in the sides of windows to act as a seal; hanging damp blankets over the doors. The study had been made into such a gas-proof room. It wasn't a very large room, 15 feet by 12 feet, say; so imagine packing in twelve blind men and a woman, two mental patients, together with Tom and myself and Mrs W.

The room was used on only one 'siren' occasion; thankfully, looking back, it was 'comic'. You see, Daddy, the very old man, slept bare, apparently he always had, and so Bob, dear fellow, gets him out of bed and slings him over his back. How on earth he did this we'll never know. However, Bob stumbles with the old man to the top of the stairhead.

Muriel, descending from the attics above, was now confronted with a naked man looking to all appearances like a live skeleton. No-one in the rush and bustle had thought to cover up the old man. Anyway, the only ones who could see him at that moment were myself and Muriel, and to my amazement she walked calmly down the stairs and into the room, to take her place on some cushions on the floor close to Pansy.

I don't remember exactly how we passed the night hours away other than that some told jokes and we sang a bit and dozed; and then it was dawn, and Tom went into the kitchen and made tea. And still we waited.

It was around seven o'clock when Tom went outside and to the gate to see if there was anyone about. There were two men on their way to work, and he remarked to them that the all-clear was a long time in going. The all-clear? they answered; that went at ten o'clock last night.

Tom called me out of the room and told me. We didn't say anything to the others. How we had missed the air-raid warning we'll never know, for apparently no-one else had heard it either, only the long all-clear at ten o'clock that, last night, we took to be the warning. But it was Muriel who had to put the cap on that long night when later in the weary day she must have slipped from her room, gone into the room where most of the men were sitting dozing and with a rolled-up piece of cardboard she walloped them all on their heads, one after the other, then marched out and up the stairs again. The noise of the men yelling had brought me running into the hall, there to see the back of her. She was still carrying her cardboard weapon. Most of the men present saw the funny side of it. Horace and Harold happened to be out, as were the little cockney lady and her husband. For this I was grateful to both parties.

The majority of my guests went to bed early, and for this I was also grateful, because by nine o'clock I could go into the drawing room and drop down into an easy chair and let out a long slow breath. I had come through another day.

That was until Bob started tapping on the door.

'Miss, would you have a look at Jimmy; he's got a boil on his, well, you know what, and he doesn't like to tell you about it. It's sore.'

Eventually I burst Jimmy's boil. It took some time.

'Miss, Dick's going to the blind-aid office in the town. He's getting bits and pieces from there. I don't know what or how much, but I thought you should know and have a word with him. You see, there's the rest of us.'

It was the first I'd heard of a blind-aid in the town. No-one from the town itself and who had anything to do with the blind had been in touch with me, and I'd had only one communication from London, and that was to say I had to take the blind, women supposedly.

Another night, another knock: 'Miss, I wonder if you'd have a look at me toe. It's been paining of late.'

'Well, you must see the doctor, Bob.'

'I'm seeing no doctors, miss, never would. No, I don't want any truck with doctors, miss.' Much shaking of the head and the shoulders. 'Just have a look at it, miss.'

'I can see it from here, Bob, and I repeat, you should go to the doctor's.'

'You did Jimmy's boil. You did that all right, miss. Look at all the stuff you go—'

'All right! All right!' I closed my eyes. 'All right! Now, sit down.'

Tom brought him a chair and a footstool on which to put his foot.

When he had taken off his sand shoe and his sock, there it was, his whole big toe exposed, and it looked awful. It was enormous.

'How on earth did you get this, Bob?'

'Gun carriage in the last war went over it, miss.'

'If that had been so,' I said sharply, 'a war hospital would have seen to you.'

'It wasn't like that at all at first, miss. It's just gone like that, you could say, over the years.'

The nail had actually become a horn. It had grown a good half-inch above the top of his actual toe, then had narrowed off, turned over and thinned out and was now embedding itself in the back of the big toe, about opposite where the base of the nail began. In growing and turning, the nail had created a sort of archway, and I could see that the space formed between the nail and the flesh was packed with something, what I didn't know. I had no implement to hand to probe it, so I asked Tom if he would go upstairs and to my dressing table where he would find the case that held a miniature button hook, a corn scalpel and a file.

A few minutes later I was probing the mass that lay under the nail. I know now I wished I hadn't, because the smell became intolerable.

However, the substance wasn't as hard as it looked and I gradually picked it out with the scalpel; and as each piece fell on to the newspaper that now covered the floor I had to turn my head away in search of a breath of different air.

When the last bit left the hole Bob almost yelled, 'Eeh! miss. Eeh! miss! Fancy that now. It's years since that was picked.'

I sat back in the chair well away from the foot and said quietly, 'Go and soak your foot now in some hot water, Bob.'

When he did not move, I said, 'You must do that; and clean out that hole.'

'Miss.'

'Yes, Bob?' My voice, I knew, was weary.

'You could file that nail off for me. You could, I know you could.'

'What!' I was sitting up straight again. 'File that nail off! I could never do that.'

'Go on, miss; you could file it off. I know you could. Ah, go on, miss. Go on.'

'Bob!' – my voice was stern now – 'you should go to the doctor or the hospital, and they would do it.'

'I'm not going to any hospital, miss. No, no; I'm not. And you could do it. Look! I'd hold me foot tight, like this. You wouldn't hurt me.' He had gripped the sole of his foot and his toes. 'And master

Tom there, he could grip my ankle to keep me foot steady. Go on, miss.'

I looked at Tom. Tom was looking down at me. Then he smiled and shook his head from side to side, before saying softly, 'You can but try. But you won't do it with your file; try this.'

He took a case from his inner pocket and from it pulled out a largish nail file and handed it to me. Then he knelt down by the foot stool and gripped Bob's ankle. With a deep intake of breath I began. Back and forth, back and forth, I pushed that file, and I could be pushing it till now for all the impression it made.

'You want a bigger file, miss.'

Yes, I wanted a larger file. I stared at Bob for some seconds. Then I looked at Tom, and to his amazement I said, 'In the workshop there are two hack-saws. Bring me the smaller one.'

'What!'

'You heard.'

'Yes, but you said . . .'

'Yes, I know what I said, he wants this nail off. I'll get no peace until it is off. Get me the hack-saw . . . please.'

From the time Tom went out till he came back with the hack-saw, Bob and I stared at each other, but said nothing. I recall the feeling in me was such as that when I was up against it: I knew that I had a fight on my hands. It had happened numerous times during the fourteen and a half years I had been in business, but those had been fights against opinions and personalities, this present one was a different kettle of fish.

My hand was quite steady as I took that hack-saw from Tom, and I did not have to give either him or Bob any further instructions, they were both gripping his foot. Slowly I drew the hack-saw across the nail towards me. Then again slowly I pushed it to the other side. It bit immediately: back and forth, back and forth, I could feel it going through. Within a matter of minutes it was done. At the front anyway. We exchanged glances.

Bob was grinning widely, Tom was smiling, and they were about to leave hold of the foot when I said, 'Wait a minute! It isn't done yet, there is the back.'

The narrow end of the nail had embedded itself in the flesh. How deep, naturally I did not know, and suddenly I was fearful. However, after giving it a slight tug it moved; and then to my utter relief the whole twisted horn fell on to my hand. And it was indeed just like the end of a ram's horn.

'Eeh! Miss Mac, you've done it. You've done it! After all these years. I never thought to see it off. You're a wonder, you know; you're a wonder.'

I lay back, for now I was feeling quite exhausted and slowly I said, 'Go and put your foot into a bowl of hot water. The skin at the back is not broken but nevertheless you must clean out where the nail was embedded. And I must say, Bob, I'll never understand why on earth you've let your toe get into this state. You could have easily gone to the hospital and they would have done just what I've done now.'

He was on his feet now stamping his bare foot up and down on the carpet almost in glee; and then he said, 'Oh, I did, miss, I did. Really, I did, but they

271

wouldn't touch it in the hospital; they said it was too dangerous to meddle with the big toe.'

'WHAT! THEY SAID WHAT!'

'Well, along those lines, miss. But anyway' – his grin was splitting his face from ear to ear – 'you've done it. Eeh! my, I can't get over it. Isn't she a wonder, Master Tom?'

Tom didn't answer. He was looking at my face because I know it had blanched.

'Goodnight, Miss Mac; and thank you from the bottom of me heart.'

'Look.' Tom was kneeling by my side. 'Don't worry; I bet he's never been near the hospital. And you know something else? I have the idea that he must have been sleeping rough for years. They do, you know, men like him. They get in small groups and they live rough, you know, underneath the arches. It's true what the song says.'

'But his sight, he must have been somewhere to see about that, that's why he's here. And surely those people would have noticed his foot and made him do something about it. He must be registered as partly blind.'

'Not necessarily. The authorities have been gathering all they could lay their hands on for evacuation. Anyway, Bob is a bit of a mystery. He doesn't seem to have any people. If he had they would surely have seen to that toe before now. Now don't worry, dear, it's off. And I think it's marvellous the way you did it. But mind, when you told me to go and get that hack-saw, well . . . but anyway, come on, get yourself up to bed; you're all in.'

On looking back, I consider the night that followed was the worst I spent during the war: my mind continuously grappled with the saying that one should never meddle with a thumb or a big toe, because the result could be lockjaw. People died from lockjaw.

It might be an old wives' tale but that night I felt it could be absolutely true. I didn't undress but sat in a chair by the side of the bed, every now and again interrupting my vigil to go and see if Bob was still breathing. My first visit was about midnight. He was lying on his back. He was neither snoring nor spluttering, his mouth was closed, and in the weak light of the dim torch he already looked dead. At his side, Daddy, the nice one, was indeed snoring and spluttering.

When a faint sigh came from Bob I retired to my room, but not to sleep, oh no; I crept downstairs and made myself a strong coffee, then returned to my post. At some time I must have dropped off for my next visit was at ten past two. Bob was still lying in the same position. He still had that dead look; he was breathing but apparently just.

Back in my room I was now seeing the headlines in the papers: they were all crude:

BOARDING-HOUSE KEEPER HACKS OFF BLIND MAN'S TOE. BLIND EVACUEE DIES AFTER LANDLADY USED A HACK-SAW TO SAW OFF HIS BIG TOE-NAIL. GUEST HOUSE OWNER USES A HACK-SAW ON THE BIG TOE-NAIL OF A BLIND EVACUEE. THE CORONER SAYS THE MAN, BOB, DIED FROM SHOCK.

On and on my thoughts raced, together with the question, why did everything seem to happen to me? All my life I had attempted to do everything for the best, and what had been my reward? Not even a day's peace. It was around half-past four in the morning when I again staggered from my room with the intention of crossing the landing. But there I bumped into a figure making for the toilet. It was Bob.

'Eeh! miss, you all right?' He peered at me in the dim light. 'Not bad or anything?'

'N-n-n-no, Bob,' I stammered; and then had a great desire to laugh, but I knew in my present state that would become hysteria.

Bob will never know how near he was to being kissed and hugged in the middle of the night by Miss Mac.

When at last I got into bed reaction set in. I couldn't sleep, I felt sick. When I did sleep I slept in, and when later I appeared downstairs weary-eyed I was greeted by all present as if I had won the war single-handed.

Some months later the order came that Hastings was to be evacuated because of the increasing threat of invasion from the sea.

The evacuees were to be moved first, and I received my second letter from the authorities, this time to ask if I could find a house in St Albans, say, and take my blind guests with me.

They must be joking. I'd had to put Pansy into hospital, poor Pansy. She looked upon The Hurst as her home. Muriel went back to her people. The first part of my war was over.

Tom and I were married on June the first. Dunkirk was being evacuated.

Shortly after this our evacuation started. The whole school was to be sent to St Albans. It was in a way the beginning of a new life, and I wasn't sorry to start it for I was very tired, very, very tired. But whenever I think back to that first year of the war and the blind, what stands out most, metaphorically speaking, is Bob's big toe.

To Laugh Or Not To Laugh

I had been asked to open the Flower Show in the White Rock Pavilion in Hastings. I hesitated whether to accept the invitation for a number of reasons. First, I hated openings because I've always thought them, in many cases, to be so unnecessary. Secondly, I had often stood feeling ridiculous like a Johnny-on-fête-days, when I've tried to throw my voice to the far end of the field where the younger ones continued to knock down coconuts and the nearer-at-hand clothes' stalls continued to do business. Thirdly, we were working like mad in the garden transporting the earth from one end of it to the other, and all on a slope of one in four, or so it seemed. We had recently laid 1,500 turves and were awaiting another 500. Lastly, it would mean my getting a new rig-out and I really couldn't afford one, although I needed one. Perhaps this was what made me finally accept.

I spent time and thought over my outfit, and the morning came when I got dressed ready for the show. The car, not ours, was coming for me at one o'clock. At twelve there was a ring at the bell. I put my head out of the window and a man said, 'I've brought your load of turves, missis. Where'll I put them?'

Oh Lord! turves at this time. 'Outside the top gate, please.'

At half-past twelve Tom came in from school. I saw him coming down our winding and very steep drive.

By now I was fully dressed in all my finery, second-hand I may say, but nevertheless very smart, and large leghorn hat. I struck a pose, and Tom looked at me, but what he said was, 'They've come!'

My pose slipped into my natural stance: 'Yes, I know,' I said flatly.

He turned from me and went hastily back up the drive, only to be stopped by my voice, like doom as I yelled, 'TOM! TOM!'

'YES?'

'HAVEN'T YOU NOTICED ANYTHING?'

From the distance he looked me up and down and said, 'Oh yes, yes; very nice; but come on' – he jerked his head – 'come and have a look at them. They're beautiful, they're straight off the marshes, and the sheep have been on them.'

Should I go in and bang the door? Should I cry? Should I laugh? I leant against the doorpost in my new creation and closed my eyes. When I opened them he was standing in front of me. 'I'm sorry,' he said; 'but they're such nice grass, they excited me.'

Well! I ask you, how can one be expected to compete with sheep-manured turves?

Another occasion when my ego was pricked was when, having been given a present of a very fetching négligé, silk coat, nightie, what there was of it, and bed jacket, I thought the time opportune to wear the nightie. I got into bed. He got into bed. He picked up a book, a maths one, of course; but I didn't pick up the *Telegraph* crossword and finish it off as I usually did; I sat up on my pillows and waited.

At one time he would read Shakespeare aloud to me and after a while I would go to sleep, but when I returned the compliment by reading Lord Chesterfield's *Letters* to him he would be breathing deeply before I ever got to the end of the first page. When that phase ended, it was maths on the male side, and the *Telegraph* crossword on the female.

But this night I had on this very special garment.

He should have noticed there was something wrong when I didn't open my mouth for the next fifteen minutes. When I did speak, my tone was chilly, to say the least.

'Why,' I asked him, 'must you always read maths books in bed?'

He turned and looked fully at me, a far-away expression on his face. Then he said softly, 'Because, dear, I find maths romantic.'

Follow that if you can.

Two Grey Birds

Two grey birds sat on a tree.
One was a he and one was a she,
And both were as plain as plain could be;
Their feathers were ruffled,
Their beaks were small,
They had no topknots on their heads at all;
But, strange to say, they were wise in a
    way,
For there passed never a day
But they found something nice to say,
He to she
And she to he:
They would compliment each other
On how lucky they were
To be able to see
The beauty in each,
He in she
And she in he.
The blackbird was blind to it,
So were the tits;
They thought that he and she
Were out of their wits.
Other birds too,
And there were more than a few,
Would have nothing to do
With that drab, bedraggled,

Sloppy pair
Sitting up there
As happy as could be,
Just thinking they could see,
She beauty in he
And he beauty in she.

I once knew a woman who was so plain that she seemed not to have one attractive feature. Yet her husband called her beautiful, and I'm sure he really thought she was. In his eyes, she must have been because they lived very happily together. They were always extolling each other, and at times this became a little sickening; but such was the impression they made on me that I wrote a short story about them. It's lying among others as yet unpublished, but who knows? when I dry up I may put them all together and bring them out as a book.

Trees

Trees can talk,
When the wind gives them tongue;
And books are bred in the mind,
When sitting beside quiet waters;
And there are many sermons to be read in
    stones:
Look at the crumbling edifices of the past,
They speak as no parson from a pulpit
    could.

Sayings

The art of talking is to know when to stop.

Tact is the Godchild of diplomacy, Diplomacy is
   the Godchild of wisdom.

Emotionally, love is an expensive business; it
   may keep you in debt all your life. Make
   sure you want to pay the interest; divorce is
   a depreciating business.

If God made the tree, why did He show me how
   to make the axe?
   Damn silly fellow! He's got no more brains
   than me.

Don't hurry to your grave, it'll wait for you.
   If you worry about it, work at it, for your
   time is short.

A Spring Day

Today the sky is high,
Today the sun shines bright;
Yesterday is forgotten;
Today my heart is light.
I think no more of tomorrow,
Or of the long night ahead,
Or the effort it has taken
To rise from my dragging bed;
For today the sky is high,
Today the sun shines bright,
And for a span, at least to me,
The whole world is right.
And all the world is in my world;
It is all about me set,
With shooting buds
And daffodils
And the promise of blossoms yet
To come and lift my spirit high,
As it is today.
For the sky is blue
And the sun shines bright
And all is right.
Tom is in the garden
Sue is at my feet,
I am the queen of all I survey
From my basket-chair seat.

Acceptance

The chapters of the year are four,
Nature has ordered it so.
They merge from one into the other:
The youth of spring growing into summer
And slowly dropping
To the heralding of its end,
Where autumn reluctantly releases it
To winter's long cold dying.
But all done with natural grace,
No fear on its face
As on mine and thine.
Lord, let me be like the tree
And end with the seasons
In dignity.

The Question II

Fast flow the rivers of my mind,
Sending to outlets and creeks
A question to the gods,
To translate the reason
That plagues the depths,
Stirring the silt
In search of the great why
I am here, only to die?
Why a waste of beauty, brawn and brain
That will never combine again,
Except in spirit?
What a thoughtless end!
Why did the gods create creation
And spread it over nation upon nation,
Only to bring it in fear to the brink?
This being their intention,
They could at least have
Denied us the power to think.

The Temperament

The night had left its film of frost;
On the moor the air was clear,
No aspic light
Between earth and cloud;
The wonder of the day
Was voiced aloud.
But suddenly apprehension flowed,
For almost in a second
Some black finger had beckoned
A pseudo night
To cover all
In a murky glow
Of hail and snow,
Driven as if by
A mighty hand,
Its purpose to demonstrate
That this is January
In Northumberland.

Fame

Their names are never mentioned in the literary lounge; they are not even skimmed over, for their writings tilt the noses of the clique.

The Queen may honour them, and they bring forth the bank managers' smiles; yet they bring forth no mention, be they commoner, lady, fellow or don.

Why?

Oh, whisper it softly, shamefully: they are best-sellers, each and every one.

The In-Between

(written in the 60s)

I do not need love or passion deep,
Or sonnets sung to lull me to sleep,
Or poems written on which my cheek will
    rest at night;
I do not need kisses on my lips
Or odes voiced to my eyes;
I do not need children about my knee
Who might grow to despise me;
I do not need prestige or power,
All of which with age go sour;
I do not need to possess another,
Claiming a debt from mother, father or
    brother;
I do not need to seek admiration in order to
    sustain life;
I do not need any of these things
For I will never be a wife,
I need only a hand to hold
In friendship,
To exchange words without spleen or hate,
To link thoughts on topics great and small,
A friend to be a metaphorical bulwark,
Or wall, against which I can lean
And draw new breath to continue the fight
    for life,

And against death,
That ultimate, that final blow
Against which all knowledge can't defend.
To that end, I only need a friend.

The Lost Man

At fifty, I had all the world could give:
A wife, a family, and a fine house in which to
    live,
Yet deep in me a want cried out
And asked what life was all about.
When I put this question to my wife and my son,
They advised a holiday, a little fun.
How could I say I have a need which cannot be
    quenched
With what I eat or see or read?
Then one day at my club I met a man to whom
    I'd never taken,
Thinking he was a reticent bore
And about character I was never mistaken.
But he cornered me and hesitantly began to talk:
I'm rich, he said; I have everything on which a
    good life depends,
Yet I am alone inside; for I can't make friends.

That was thirty years ago;
Now, our heads are like snow.
But the port is good and our cigars draw well,
And the fire is aglow.

Morning Colours

There are jewels on the lawn,
Diamonds and pearls; no rubies alas,
For that jewel creates only pale hues on the
  grass.
Yet on the cobwebs hanging between the
  leaves
We get amethysts, garnets, and rubies too,
And golden threads heavy with dew.
The canvas in nature's studio dazzles and
  beguiles the artist's eye,
But only through memory can he supply
A picture to embrace the art of the morning
  dew.

Lonely Woman

Darkened windows in the street,
Footsteps like ghostly boots minus feet;
A stray wind, rebel from the storm of the
    day,
Shakes the house
And clears a path for the rain,
Each ping a note played on glass.
The dirge repeated,
Echoes it will pass,
For the night is a microscope,
Created to enlarge sorrow
And loneliness; a planet
On to which women without men
Have been banished
And men without 'the woman'
In similar plight.
    God send the morror
And save us from the night.

The Short Silence

In the silence of the snow
No songbird shivers the white glow,
No adverse thought
In the silence of the snow.

Embalmed, I stand,
No memory of the past;
I have reached the ultimate at last
In the silence of the snow.

No thought of the future
And the thaw
That will turn the white to grey,
Come day;
Enough to know
I've experienced this moment
In the silence of the snow.

I experienced this moment when standing in the garden of Bristol Lodge, Northumberland.

It was as if I had been drawn out of the house in order to feel this silence. The only other time comparable with this was on a 'road' in a pit (mine), down which I had been taken by my cousin, Peter Lavelle, in order to experience the workings of a mine. He had put out his lamp and said, 'Listen!'

The blackness scared me to death, but more still did the silence affect me; not with joy this time, but with pure terror. This was real nothingness.

The Donkey

If your plan is, Lord,
That I return to life,
Please don't send me back
As a donkey.
As a human, I've been well acquainted
With pain and strife,
But never to the extent
Meted out to a donkey or a mule,
For that state would be too cruel:
No way of protesting
Against the prong,
Or the burden, the neglect,
The body sores, the tortured hoof,
Only to hang the head in mute reproof.

What harm has that little animal ever
    done to man
That he should reward it so?
All it asks for its labours
Is a bite, a bed, and a show of love.
So pity me and heed my plea:
Don't return me as a donkey,
For I may not be so lucky,
As eventually to end my days
In that donkey heaven
In Devon.

That Element

The wind has raged all day,
Tearing at the trees,
Deluding dead winter leaves
Into dancing life
By its whistling roaring voice.
Even the clouds have no choice
But to scurry and twist
And aim to rise high,
Until in vexatious retaliation
They call on the rain
To cool its capers.

So, like a child,
I picture the elements
And ask from where did they come?
To where do they go?
And why can I only see
Their destruction.
The rain, the fog, the mist, the snow,
All these I know,
But the wind that tears the sea,
Like God,
Is a frightening mystery,
Both to the child and me.

Such a Day

(Thursday 14 October 1988)

From where has this day crept?
Like a sweet calm gentle stranger from
    another plane?
Did yesterday go mad with wind and
    rain?
How came this day of grace
Which has washed from my face
The sullen air,
And where yesterday was despair
Now there is content
And appreciation and hope
That warmth, calmness and sunlight
    bring?
Would that an Indian Summer come in
    Winter too,
For dream days like this are too few.

PART THREE

My Private War

Words

The relationship between Tom and me has grown with the years. I think the secret is, we talk: apart from everyday events, we discuss things. For example, one morning last week, around six o'clock, he got up and made a cup of tea, and as we sat drinking it he remarked casually, 'Odd, Mrs So-and-So saying you are an existentialist.' By the way, this Mrs So-and-So was a master's wife and a brilliant woman who was kind enough not only to read me but also to express her liking of my work. Tom added, 'You've rejected most tags, but retained those of an agnostic and a storyteller. What exactly is an existentialist?'

Neither of us could give a clear definition, so he got up and raked out reference books and from the hyperbole we were asked to understand that an existentialist believes that existence comes before essence.

Oh, was that it? Now I knew what I was! I knew where I stood as clearly as if I were in a thick fog on Dartmoor.

Anyway, once again it set us off discussing and probing: Was there any truth in such an obscure statement? And what was truth anyway? So you see, there lies the secret of our marriage. We are not only husband and wife, and I'm not only mother and mistress to him and he lover and help-mate in all ways to me, we are friends, and real friends accept each other's faults, and we have plenty of these to exchange. Moreover, friends like each other; and there is the operative word, LIKE.

But to pick up that word 'truth'. Well, to use a common phrase, it's always bugged me because, who dares to speak it anyway? And when it is supposedly spoken it is only one man's opinion; all right, a number of opinions of others put together, but it is still fallible.

For my part, I think a white lie is as near to the so-called truth that I want to come. A white lie is kind, the supposed truth is so often cruel. It can wreck a marriage, a home, even a country.

Politicians are good examples of white liars. Well, if they spoke the truth they would never get in, would they, because then they would have to admit that 75 per cent of their endeavour was in seeking personal power.

I think one of the sweet words of our language is diplomacy. Think of the trouble a diplomat could start if he stepped out of pattern and spoke the truth in a foreign country.

I've spoken of words. I'm frustrated by them or, more correctly, by their meaning. As one gets to my age certain words take on deep significance, such as . . . God and death. Do you know, I used to be terrified of that word 'death'. I shied from it because it would keep me awake at night probing, asking questions to which there have never been any answers, only those contrived through imagery and fear, such as heaven and hell. But now I can think of death with only slight apprehension and, on the other hand, a great deal of interest. The apprehension concerns being parted from Tom, the interest lies in the fact that, as I see it now, if there is anything after death – and I dismiss the many mansions on one hand and eternal punishment on the other – then whatever there is could turn out to be a great adventure. I only hope it isn't reincarnation because I might then be sent back as somebody worse than I am now, and I have enough trouble with my present self, I can tell you.

One thing that makes me sad when I think about my demise is the blotting out of this box up here, one's brain. What a waste if there's nothing over there. To think that this wonderful piece of machinery which is beyond man's conception but which can take him back to the beginning of time, and imagine the future, besides giving him a consciousness and a subconsciousness and a mass of desires and emotions, is going to be thrown into the void of oblivion. If I had to accept this theory, then the Creator of it, which is commonly called God, has, according to the workings of the mind He has given me, slipped up badly somewhere.

No, I reject that, but what I do believe is that this remarkable piece of grey matter that I have been loaned will return from where it came and join a central power.

Anyway, this is just my opinion, but it is a comfort to me that I can say with Descartes, I think, so I exist.

Look Here Now

'Tis Sunday again.
Come on, Katie, be kind,
Leave God alone for today,
He's got a lot on His mind:
The baddies, the goodies and the neither-
     here-nor-theres;
The ones that say He isn't,
And those that say He is,
And those who tell they can feel His touch:
Oh! that lot.
I believe them not.
But if it helps them to get through a day
Who am I to say,
Give over, face up to reason;
That will make you see?
For, after all, what has reason done for me,
But go into battle each Sunday from
     breakfast to tea,
When this same reason tells me He isn't
     there,
Or anywhere, that I can see?
Which certainly gives me the lie,
Especially today, I've let Him pass by.
I wonder if He'll miss me,
Or take the huff and let me go my way.
I hope He doesn't, you know, but we'll see.

Sunday, 12 February 1989

Talking with Him again after another Sunday morning listening to the religious programme.

Look here! Why are You hiding Your face?
Let's put our cards on the table:
You admit that Almighty prefixes Your name,
So, if that is the case,
What, may I ask,
Are You doing about Your human race?
For it's in a hell of a state!
There are wars, massacres, tortures and rape;
And Your Church has been split in two
From the hem to the nape.
Jesus is stripped bare as if on the Cross,
Christianity is getting nowhere fast
And is now a commercial do:

Listen to Sky disc and I'll pray for you;
Everything you want you can have,
If you believe as I do.
But we've got to live, you know,
So send your donations just to show
You believe in God.

Well! What do you say to such a mess?
. . . What! Man is in Your image no less?

And You've given him free will
And it's up to him how he uses it?
Oh, don't give me that pill,
And that You have Your ways to sort him out,
With pestilence, plagues and drought.

Yes, as you say, Katie,
With pestilence and plagues and drought,
But AIDS, Man has himself brought about.
Volcanic eruptions, blizzards, snow and ice, I
    also own,
But this is nothing to what man himself
    condones:
He has poisoned the atmosphere and the sea;
He has wiped out the forests, the wildlife too,
And, what is more, millions in war.

And for his gods he has chosen
Gold and Power.
And so, you see,
My face is not hidden from your planet;
My gaze is wide.
And, Katie, like yours,
My heart is sore.

The Long Sleep

I will not question more,
I will not ask the reason why,
I'll simply wait for the answer
Until the day I die.
And if I find an empty space,
A mere wilderness of time,
And no-one there to answer
The sky-shattering question why
I was born merely to enable me to die,
I will not rage or weaken
But remain still within the shroud
And quietly and resignedly,
Amid the mighty silent
And unseen crowd,
Sleep.

Be Still

Be still my thoughts
On God and life.
Be still my thoughts
On my early strife.
Be still the bitterness
I still hold strong,
Be still the retribution
I crave for the wrong
That brought me into this world
And then
Gave me an early taste of hell,
Accentuated by sensitivity.
Too much, too much;
Emotions gone wild
When set against the norm
Of a child.
Then into youth,
Attacking truth
With untried false-valued reason,
That sped into adulthood
Unseasoned with faith or hope;
And on into valiant age
Ignorance,
Like a mountain spate enraged,
Spewed from the tongue
Until the mirror of the mind,

On the fast-approaching end,
Looked with awe
And saw
The days flying fast
And the past
Enveloped in a few words:
If you want peace,

BE STILL.

The Price

Why do we always have to pay for love?
God above, I ask you,
Why do we always have to pay for love?
The final payment is parting,
And a hundred per cent is too high;
I am bankrupt with emotion at the thought;
I, too, would want to die.

Why am I whining?
I have not yet been crucified.
Did He not say, on that mangled tree,
God above, why charge me
This fearful price for love?

Why must love be the dearest commodity?

Pain

Do we learn from pain?
Is there anything in it at all that we gain?
Are we better people because we bleed?
Is disease of any kind what we need
To cleanse our soul
And make us whole,
A human being as God intended?
Are our spirits uplifted,
Our days bright, our nights
One long sweet dream passage through
    sleep?
Do we wake to greet another day
And while pain-racked, do we say, 'tis good
    to be alive:
I must strive to appreciate the sun, the light;
I must not think about my plight
But count the benefits of the day,
At any rate,
Fight no more against the grain?
DO WE?
DO WE?
No; we learn nothing from pain,
We can only reckon up the sum of life
With
What can't be cured must be endured.

The Soul

Where is my soul?
It occupies no space:
No corner, no shelf.
I am whole,
I am one,
Complete in my mind,
But where is my soul?
What substance does it contain?
What makes its feelings sustain me
Through pain?
I don't know;
I can only look to my spirit again.
The answer is no.
Then what is my soul?
Something that was before me
But will be again when my body is no
    more?
Will the I in me soar with it into another
    realm
Once I leave the tomb?
I appeal to the endless sky,
And the answer is:
You're right about one thing,
You won't know until you die.

Nothing is For Ever

Nothing is for ever:
Death begins at birth,
The span between a lottery,
Chance . . . long straw or short.

Nothing is for ever:
Forests mould into coal,
Icebergs melt,
And volcanoes burn themselves out.

Nothing is for ever:
The sun, the moon have a span,
Stars burn out,
And rivers cease to run.

If nothing is for ever,
Why have I collected a home?
And treasured bits and pieces in each
    room;
Why have I put money in the bank,
And striven for recognition and rank?

Is it because that power out there
Has given to mankind
A brain out of which comes thought
In order to recognise all He has wrought

And the power to wonder at His might?
Perhaps! But it's a poor answer.
So still I search for light
To penetrate the right
Of life.

From the Opaque to the Agony

I dream a lot but no longer do I dream of being imprisoned in a rock-bound valley and of struggling up a sheer cliff face, only to reach an overhang at the top, and know I cannot surmount it, and wake up gasping and in a lather of sweat. That dream faded when my first novel *Kate Hannigan* was accepted.

And I no longer dream of fighting my mother, beating her, struggling madly with her; that dream vanished twelve years after she died, on the completion of my autobiography. The autobiography, as I have said, had perforce to cover a period of twelve years during which I rewrote it eight times, deleting a little bitterness with each attempt, but the process was very therapeutic for me.

And I no longer dream of flying, sometimes taking off in the street stark naked and wondering why nobody notices me; sometimes just saying to myself, 'Go on, fly,' and watching myself rise from the ground whilst experiencing the most ecstatic feeling of pleasure. It was said that the flying dream was connected with sex, and so it could be interpreted that, now I no longer dream of flying, my sex life is over. Well, I can explode that theory once and for all.

My dream last night had been of running downstairs, hundreds and hundreds of stairs, then turning a corner and thinking I'd reached the bottom, and there they were, more stairs, flight after flight. I woke up in the dark and life lay on me like the deep night, black and heavy, no small glimmer of light in it, and the question that must have evolved when the first probing brain cells came into my mind, Why?

Why strive to live?

What was life for?

I have periods when this question comes at me with hammer blows and I aim to ward it off, using the escape routes, and think of God, all the gods of men, good work, travel, enjoyment. But I have found these to be less than useless; in my case there is only one cure against depression, work.

Yet there are times, as last night, when my body has been too tired to answer my brain and get me out of bed and to my desk, and so I lie and ask myself the final why? Why even bother to write? Is my writing worth a tuppenny damn? When I reach this point I am desperate.

I put my hand out to touch Tom. He wasn't there. He must have got up with yet another migraine headache.

I went downstairs. 'How are you feeling?' I said.

'Oh, a little better. Why are you up?'

'I've got the blues.'

'Then there's a pair of us. Come on, we'll have a cup of tea.'

In the kitchen, close to the Aga, we sat and asked of each other the same question, why? Why a mathematician and a writer living in a beautiful house, set in a beautiful garden and dearly, dearly beloved of each other, should be tormented so, and the conclusion we came to was that our condition was not apparently just of one thing but a combination of many. On my side, the sensitivity of the artist, the agonising sensitivity of awareness: the awareness of the pain of life, the awareness of the fears on which happiness is built, the sensitivity that gives sharp outlines to life and strips off layers of skin and makes one vulnerable to the sting of the unkind word, even to the lowering of a supercilious eyelid.

And in Tom, the sensitivity of the idealist coupled with a rapier-sharp critical mind, a thoughtful gentle creature who gives the impression to the world that he is of a quiet, placid, self-effacing nature, when incongruously he is more often than not burnt up inside about causes, injustice and people, both those really in need and those who want something for nothing, the moral twisters he calls them, those good folk who smirk as they say, 'Well, everybody's doing it, and if I don't have it somebody else will. There's so much fallen off the lorries, there's hardly anything left to be delivered these days, so if you can't beat 'em join 'em.'

I said I felt guilty at experiencing such despair while I still had him. He said he felt the same way.

This scourge deep within us is the result of pressures, in my case fifty years of them, in his the struggle to make a compromise between a working-class background and a pre-war university education.

And then there's the little things, stupid little things that happened in childhood to us both and which, buried deep, grow with the years almost into phobias. In Tom's case one such makes me angry now when I think of it. How stupid some parents are, especially mothers who keep repeating some episode which they considered extremely funny.

Tom was brought up in a happy home; his mother loved him dearly, in fact he was the apple of her eye, there was no-one to compare with her Tom, so it wasn't with malice that she repeated again and again over the years that when he had been born his father had looked at him and exclaimed, 'My God! isn't he ugly. Did you ever see a mouth like that?' And she would go on to relate that when the dog looked at him it dashed out of the room and was never seen again.

I love to laugh and there's nothing does one more good than a real belly laugh, and I noticed over the years that when Tom laughed he made no sound, he kept his lips closed. I once said to him, 'You don't enjoy laughter,' but he assured me he did but that he laughed inwardly.

It is a comparatively few years ago that he told me it was because of this oft-repeated tale he didn't open his mouth wide when he laughed, and so there had built up within him frustrations and inhibitions with which he did not come to terms for many years.

But even when you do come to terms with these mental sores and you heal them with right thinking, the scars remain, and in both our cases the scars resulted in bouts of depression.

As we talked we felt better. We drank our tea, we kissed, we went upstairs, our hands holding tight, and then to bed. The night was not so black now. It would soon be dawn, and day.

The next morning we smiled at each other. I

looked at the piece of paper on the bedside table and the lines I had scribbled in the dark. The lines read:

Why fear dying when living is nothing but an open wound.

Did I feel as bad as that last night?

The sun is shining – I think I've got an idea for a new story.

The Answer

I've often wondered about the answer to prayer
Regarding pain and suffering.
I've wondered at times if God was there.
I've asked, Why me?
I'm not bad,
Maybe not all that good,
Just a sort of in-between grey.
But You have supposedly made me,
I would have thought You understood.
Yet I seem to be paying too much for my life.
Tell me, why have You loaded me with this
    sickness and strife?

Yet it hadn't struck me before when I read my
    mail,
Each letter thanking me in detail,
That I'd been given a gift. The power to use
    which
Had in a way my ails diffused.
For, never would I have had time to write,
Had I not been tied to this bed from noon till
    night.

It seems that He never gives a straight answer
    to so-called prayer.

The Video of Man's Conception of God

As a child, I saw You:
There You were watching me running
   wild
Within the compounds of the Church
Promising me heaven;
And hell, too,
Should I not believe in You.

As a girl, more steady now, and thinking
But fearful still,
I was forced to do Thy will,
Wanting to believe
While pushing against the man-made
   deity.

Then I, the young woman,
Dared to question Your omnipotent will,
And war began:
The video God became a menace;
I no longer believe in penance
So breached the wall and was free
Like wind, sea or air, free, free.

This being so, why was I still tormented?
Why did You follow me?
Through wind, sea and air

Until my mind, crazed with doubts
Dared to shout,
'Look! Can't You see I've thrown You out?'

Slowly You faded from my sight.
The video face out I wiped
With lines of reason
Which deepened with the season
Of the year.
But then I found
Reason doesn't conquer thought,
Nor bring the peace
For a lifetime sought.

But why has it taken an age
To admit I hunger still,
Not for the compound and the Church's
    double face,
Or for the Fathers so full of grace,
But for the Friend
Who has stood on the sideline
And whom I, the referee,
Refused to see?

Is it too late
To hold out my hand and say,
Where e'er You are
I wish to be
Nearer, my Friend, to Thee?
As it was in the beginning,
Is now
And ever shall be,
All is mystery.

That Man

How do I view You,
Supposed Son of God?
As a clean-shaven, pale-faced Hebrew?
Like this, You would have stood out
Among them, wouldn't You?
Not forgetting Your robes white as snow.

Or the new version?
A small man,
Still without a beard
But dark of brow,
And fiery-eyed.
But like this, You would be
Acceptable only to a few,
For in the main
The handsome man would win,
Especially in the female gene.
SO AGAIN WHERE DOES THIS LEAD
    ME?
Have I to contrive, in the shadows,
Another vision to be plagued by
This irritation of history,
This mystery man,
Who has caused more havoc than all the
    despots
Up to this day?

One of us must win,
The shadow or I?
But what a pity
That only through time and death
Will the answer come
From beyond the boundless sky.

God is a Hippopotamus

I have always talked to my inner self, but the idea of talking to an animal, asking it questions and getting answers that I certainly didn't want but which I knew were absolutely right, took on the appearance of normality after I read an article about Dr Art Ulene who had written a book called *Feeling Fine*, a simple, amusing, yet profound and helpful book on how to pull oneself together through one's own efforts.

From the article I learned that the choosing of an animal to talk to was part of the therapeutic process of keeping mentally, and physically, healthy. The author himself did it, his family did it, and countless television viewers followed his advice.

But what animal did I choose?

I chose a hippo.

Why?

I don't know; perhaps because he is an ugly, ungainly, unfriendly beast. Nevertheless, I would conjure up a deserted sandy beach backed by scrub, out of which would lumber towards me this huge animal and slowly flop down by my side.

I am always the first to speak, pouring out my troubles and asking him what I should do about them. In a very short while I learned that he proffered no easy way out, he was no appeaser giving me the answers I wanted to hear. More often than not he would be pointing out my deviousness, obstinacy, cowardice or aggressiveness; and were I to attempt to justify my reasons, he would pull himself up and walk away, saying, 'Well, you know what's right; it's up to you.'

I am an agnostic. I am continually probing; consequently, I am lonely inside. When I left the Catholic Church I left the comfort and protection of the compound in which I was allowed unlimited freedom: I could lie, drink, bash out, hate or whore if I were so inclined, knowing that I would be forgiven after confessing my sins. But what I found I wasn't allowed to do was to let my mind jump the boundary and wander among new thoughts, because when it returned to the compound it questioned. So I revolted, and there was nothing for it but I had to leave the shelter of the compound and life everlasting.

The wilderness is an awesome place, vast, frightening and so lonely. The mind can't cope with it; it breaks down and you become mentally blind and wander around in circles, perhaps for years.

Eventually, after great trauma, I came across a path that showed a little light, but it led away from all doctrines, and definitely from that being called God. But there was this Jesus. Well, I could conceive that he was a good man, but not God-made man. No. Nevertheless I read about him, and could believe many things he said, such as 'The Kingdom of God is within you', upon which I put my own interpretation, meaning that all the power you needed to get through this life was ready and waiting for you to tap.

326

Fair enough; but how to get at it? I had to find a key or a bottle opener to let the genie out, so I read. I read every type of book, including the Bible, from where I thought I might get a lead; but to no avail.

Then one day, when I'd reached the depth, my being called out for help. I wanted to talk to someone with my mind, for there were thoughts I couldn't put into words, even to the one closest to me, my husband. I wanted someone to understand my need before I voiced it, even before my conscious mind grappled with it. It was then that I read *Feeling Fine*; and the idea of making a confidant of an animal appealed to me. I saw myself sitting on this lonely stretch of beach and in conversation with a hippo. Afterwards I thought that should I tell anyone I would be considered barmy. Over the years when I've laughingly spoken of this, I have gleaned that my statement had been a foregone conclusion.

Even when I was aware that I wasn't alone in my lunacy, there were times when I asked myself why I resorted to this outlet. Then one day, quite recently, I received the answer: I asked my hippo outright why I should have chosen him to be the receptacle of my woes, why, when I wanted the truth, did I conjure him up? even though I knew his answers to my questions would cause me to take the most difficult line. What he said amounted to: I, being of a probing, self-opinionated and stubborn nature, always aiming to be different, could not accept God as Christians do through Christ, or as Moslems do, Muhammad, or as the Chinese derive their wisdom through Confucius, but, as I'd found my spiritual being, yet would not openly acknowledge it, other than

327

through the camouflage of an animal, well, that was all right with Him. He didn't mind in the least appearing as a hippo; hippos were dignified, fearless animals. Anyway, as He said, the main thing was we now understood each other and He hoped that, as I now also understood I wasn't just talking to myself, I wouldn't send Him packing back into the scrub, or ask Him to inhabit a more lovable beast; and further, that, having found comfort from my spiritual help, I would not shy away from the mystery of the Omnipotent One who could spread Himself, even into the bulk of a mud-coated hippopotamus, in order to have a word with me, but would try to understand and come to believe, that with God, all things were possible, and that there was no channel too dark or too ugly through which He would not travel in order to reach me. So be it!

Knowledge II

It was at twenty years of age and working in the South Shields workhouse when I first read Lord Chesterfield's *Letters To His Son*, and as I have said before, I was both surprised and disturbed by the knowledge of my ignorance. I realised I knew nothing. I had been nowhere. I also realised that I thought I knew much more than those with whom I worked. I hid my ignorant superiority under laughter and self-deprecation while all the time imagining that, having been bred of this unknown father, the gentleman, I was bound to be different.

It wasn't a pleasant awakening to self and it actually didn't come overnight, for the further I read into this man's letters, the snobbery and the egotism I won't say passed me by, rather that at times I felt one with them. However, what the *Letters* did do for me was to make me think and read.

My thinking might still have a horizon but my reading opened doors in my mind of which I'd never been aware even as I walked through them into the complexities of another's thinking.

I wasn't really aware that I was learning when I read history. I was, though, aware that nothing seemed to have altered: people thought, argued, probed, fought and killed each other, often in terrible ways: it was repetition, repetition all down the ages, slaughter, mostly in the name of God.

At one point I asked myself why I went on: the more I read the more disturbed I became. Knowledge, I was finding, didn't bring happiness, not even contentment. And this was the state of my mind when I left the North for the South; nor have all the years of probing since brought about any significant change, for, at eighty-five, I know that knowledge is not a substitute for what, in my case, should have been my main aim in life, and I suppose still is: peace of mind.

Why?

How wonderful for some
Who by faith know from the start
That Christ is in their heart:
No probing;
No battles;
No rage;
Just an uncomplicated faith for all to see.
So I ask:
Why not me?
The answer I suppose is yet to come:
When totted up and placed before the
    auditor,
The sum of my term
Will state the reason why,
Perhaps to say
Her lack of faith has been through strife
And probing the reason of life.

Silence

Be still and know I am the silence;
Be still and know I am the wind, the rain and
    the volcanic power;
Be still and know I am the dawn, the sunset,
    the night;
Be still and know I am the heavens above
In which I have made the light that cannot be
    fathomed;
Be still and know that I am time, I am the
    minute and the hour;
Be still and know that I have more than one son,
    the universe sprang from my bed;
Be still and know that I love you in sin and I
    love you in sorrow, I love you in pain and
    share your fear of tomorrow;
Nothing is unknown to me from pole to pole,
So rest in silence
Knowing I am your soul.

LET ME MAKE MYSELF PLAIN
by Catherine Cookson

In *Let Me Make Myself Plain* Catherine Cookson may be said to break new ground as an author. The title echoes her first surprised reaction to a television producer's suggestion that she undertake a series of late-night Epilogues. She accepted the challenge with results so successful that many who heard the talks wrote asking for their publication.

Here they form the core of a remarkable collection of essays and the poems she modestly describes as 'prose on short lines', into which she has distilled over the years a deeply personal and hard-won philosophy. Uncompromisingly honest and free of illusion, but with an ultimate message of hope and encouragement, the book is imbued with characteristic down-to-earth common sense and humour.

Whether writing of priests or doctors, or looking back to eisodes in her Tyneside childhood, she constantly displays all the qualities that have made her one of the world's most widely-read and best-loved novelists.

0 552 13407 4

CATHERINE COOKSON COUNTRY
by Catherine Cookson

Catherine Cookson was born in 1906 into the bleak industrial heartland of Tyneside, and rose to become one of the most successful novelists of all time.

Life on the south bank of the Tyne was hard, often cruel, vicious and rough; and for Catherine and her unmarried mother, doubly so.

In *Catherine Cookson Country* she returns to her homeland, the landscape which provides the setting for her novels. And in the company of her best-loved fictional characters she rediscovers its human contours: the feelings, emotions and fiercely held passions which inspired her as woman and writer.

0 552 13126 1

OUR KATE
by Catherine Cookson

Catherine Cookson is known and loved for her vibrant and earthy novels set in and around the North-east of England, past and present. Her auto-biography makes plain how it is she knows her background and her characters so well.

The Our Kate of the title is not Catherine Cookson, but her mother, around whom the autobiography revolves. Despite her faults, Kate emerges as a warm and loveable human figure.

Our Kate is an honest statement about living with hardship and poverty, seen through the eyes of a highly sensitive child and woman, whose zest for life and unquenchable sense of humour won through to make Catherine Cookson the warm, engaging and human writer she is today.

0 552 14093 7

A SELECTION OF OTHER CATHERINE COOKSON TITLES AVAILABLE FROM CORGI BOOKS

THE PRICES SHOWN BELOW WERE CORRECT AT THE TIME OF GOING TO PRESS. HOWEVER, TRANSWORLD PUBLISHERS RESERVE THE RIGHT TO SHOW NEW RETAIL PRICES ON COVERS WHICH MAY DIFFER FROM THOSE PREVIOUSLY ADVERTISED IN THE TEXT OR ELSEWHERE.

13576 3	THE BLACK CANDLE	£5.99
12473 7	THE BLACK VELVET GOWN	£5.99
14063 5	COLOUR BLIND	£4.99
12551 2	A DINNER OF HERBS	£5.99
14066 X	THE DWELLING PLACE	£4.99
14068 6	FEATHERS IN THE FIRE	£4.99
14089 9	THE FEN TIGER	£4.99
14069 4	FENWICK HOUSES	£4.99
10450 7	THE GAMBLING MAN	£4.99
13716 2	THE GARMENT	£4.99
13621 2	THE GILLYVORS	£4.99
10916 9	THE GIRL	£4.99
14071 6	THE GLASS VIRGIN	£4.99
13685 9	THE GOLDEN STRAW	£5.99
13300 0	THE HARROGATE SECRET	£5.99
14087 2	HERITAGE OF FOLLY	£4.99
13303 5	THE HOUSE OF WOMEN	£4.99
10780 8	THE IRON FAÇADE	£4.99
13622 0	JUSTICE IS A WOMAN	£4.99
14091 0	KATE HANNIGAN	£4.99
14092 9	KATIE MULHOLLAND	£5.99
14081 3	MAGGIE ROWAN	£4.99
13684 0	THE MALTESE ANGEL	£4.99
13088 5	THE PARSON'S DAUGHTER	£4.99
14073 2	PURE AS THE LILY	£4.99
13683 2	THE RAG NYMPH	£4.99
14075 9	THE ROUND TOWER	£4.99
13714 6	SLINKY JANE	£4.99
10541 4	THE SLOW AWAKENING	£4.99
10630 5	THE TIDE OF LIFE	£5.99
14038 4	THE TINKER'S GIRL	£4.99
12368 4	THE WHIP	£4.99
13577 1	THE WINGLESS BIRD	£5.99
13247 0	THE YEAR OF THE VIRGINS	£4.99
13126 1	CATHERINE COOKSON COUNTRY	£9.99
14093 7	OUR KATE	£4.99
13407 4	LET ME MAKE MYSELF PLAIN	£4.99

All Transworld titles are available by post from:
Book Service By Post, PO box 29, Douglas, Isle of Man IM99 1BQ
Credit cards accepted. Please telephone 01624 675137, fax 01624 670923 or Internet http://www. bookpost.co.uk for details.
Please allow £0.75 per book for post and packing UK.
Overseas customers allow £1 per book for post and packing.